YA

W9-BNO-443

MADONNA
G NU

Madonna

"Express Yourself"

Read about other
American REBELS

Jack Kerouac
"The Road Is Life"

ISBN-13: 978-0-7660-2448-9
ISBN-10:   0-7660-2448-2

Jimi Hendrix
"Kiss The Sky"

ISBN-13: 978-0-7660-2449-6
ISBN-10:   0-7660-2449-0

James Dean
*"Dream As If You'll
Live Forever"*

ISBN-13: 978-0-7660-2537-0
ISBN-10:   0-7660-2537-3

Kurt Cobain
*"Oh Well, Whatever,
Nevermind"*

ISBN-13: 978-0-7660-2426-7
ISBN-10:   0-7660-2426-1

Madonna

" Express Yourself "

Carol Gnojewski

 Enslow Publishers, Inc.
40 Industrial Road
Box 398
Berkeley Heights, NJ 07922
USA
http://www.enslow.com

*To my brothers Mike and Steve (who first introduced
me to Madonna) and brother-in-law Dan, whose courage and
example have challenged my understanding of gender roles.
And to Conrad and Gary for moral support.*

Library of Congress Cataloging-in-Publication Data

Gnojewski, Carol.
  Madonna : "express yourself" / Carol Gnojewski.
    p. cm. — (American rebels)
  Includes bibliographical references and index.
  ISBN-13: 978-0-7660-2442-7
  ISBN-10: 0-7660-2442-3
  1. Madonna, 1958–   —Juvenile literature. 2. Rock musicians—United
States—Biography—Juvenile literature. 3. Motion picture actors and actresses—
United States—Biography—Juvenile literature. I. Title. II. Title: Express yourself.
ML3930.M26G66 2008
782.42166092—dc22
[B]
                                                        2006025993

Printed in the United States of America

10 9 8 7 6 5 4 3 2

To Our Readers: We have done our best to make sure all Internet Addresses in this
book were active and appropriate when we went to press. However, the author and
the publisher have no control over and assume no liability for the material available
on those Internet sites or on other Web sites they may link to. Any comments or
suggestions can be sent by e-mail to comments@enslow.com or to the address on
the back cover.

Every effort has been made to locate all copyright holders of material used in this
book. If any errors or omissions have occurred, corrections will be made in future
editions of this book.

Illustration Credits: Associated Press, pp. 10, 12, 31, 81, 84, 90, 92,
108, 120, 125; Associated Press, Graylock, p. 133; Classmates Media,
Inc., pp. 35, 39.

Cover Illustration: Associated Press.

Contents

1 I Feel It in Your Kiss 7

2 What It Feels Like for a Girl 15

3 Mother and Father 21

4 Papa Don't Preach 27

5 Causing a Commotion 33

6 You Can Dance, for Inspiration 37

7 You'll See 43

8 Gambler 48

9 Born to Be Alive 51

10 Madonna in the Sky 56

11 Right on Track 60

12 Everybody, Everybody 63

13 Starlight, Star Bright 67

14 Keep on Pushin' Me 70

15 Burning Up 74

16 Why's It So Hard 79

17 Poison Penns 86

18 I Can Feel Your Power 93

Contents

19 Live Out Your Fantasies
Here With Me 100

20 A League of Her Own 107

21 You Must Love Me 113

22 Open Your Heart to Me 118

23 Time Goes So Slowly 127

Selected Discography 138

Chapter Notes 140

Further Reading
(Books and Internet Addresses) 156

Index 158

I Feel It in Your Kiss

I always wanted the biggest piece of the cake.
—Madonna[1]

It is September 1984, well into what historians refer to as the "go-go" decade due to an obsession with personal wealth, accompanied by an increase in production and consumer spending. Corporate culture reigns supreme, coining clever acronyms to aspire to. It's hip, for example, to be a YUPPIE (Young Urban Professional) with lots of disposable income, or if married, a DINK (Double Income No Kids).

Home computers are a rarity and video recording technology is in its infancy. Sales for Sony Betamax home video cassette recorders, first marketed in 1975, peak globally at 2.3 million units. They will soon lose ground to rival video format VHS (Video Home System), sparking the new phenomenon of video rental stores.[2] Republican president Ronald Reagan, a former actor turned politician known as the Great Communicator for his effective use of the dominant medium of television, resides in the White House.

Pioneer music-video cable network MTV holds the first annual Video Music Awards (VMA). This inaugural ceremony, broadcast live on MTV from New York's Radio City Music Hall, parodies the Grammy Awards with irreverent stunts and surprise appearances by music industry professionals. Hosted by Bette Midler, it is the first awards show to honor the achievements of the innovative artists who helped to shape the fledgling music-video format since the network's emergence three years earlier in the summer of 1981. Winners receive "Moon Men," small statues of an astronaut on the moon. One of the earliest MTV logos incorporated images of space exploration, symbolizing the network's innovative and exploratory nature.

During the show, superstar Michael Jackson wins the Viewer's Choice Award for "Thriller," the first long-form video shown on MTV. The fourteen-minute video, ten minutes longer than average, tells the story of a couple whose date takes a surreal turn when they cut through a graveyard on their way home from a horror movie. Jackson, the first major black artist to appear on MTV, revolutionized the concept of the music video and set the bar in terms of performance and production quality with extravaganzas like "Thriller," incorporating storytelling and lavishly choreographed dance sequences. Previously, record companies conceived these videos as low-budget promotional items.

Alongside Jackson, other award-winners that evening include the Cars for "You Might Think," Cyndi Lauper for "Girls Just Want To Have Fun," the Eurythmics for "Sweet Dreams (Are Made of This)," David Bowie for "China Girl," Herbie Hancock for "Rockit," and ZZ Top for "Legs." But the highlight of the show is the now-classic performance of a young, upcoming vocalist named Madonna, previewing her sophomore album with a live rendition of the soon to be chart-topping, "Like a Virgin."

Strands of white lights form twinkling rainbow arches above a gigantic three-tiered wedding cake with a life-size bride and groom as the cake topper. As the music begins, the bride steps forward and lifts her veil. Underneath is Madonna, clad in

The highlight of the show is the now-classic performance of a young, upcoming vocalist.

white lace gloves that hug her muscular upper arms, and a sexy bridal dress with a white, lace bustier top. A leather belt that reads "Boy Toy" holds up her tulle skirt, sprinkled with polka dot hearts. Boy Toy, she later explained, is her graffiti tag name.[3] It also became the name of her company and that of a clothing collection featuring Madonna-inspired fashions. To her tongue-in-cheek sensibility, the moniker meant, "I toy with boys."

Madonna descends the white staircase built into the cake, crucifix necklaces swinging. She sweetly sings

Madonna's performance at the 1984 MTV Video Music Awards was not only the highlight of the show, but also a catalyst for her rapid rise to stardom.

about past relationships and finding true love. As the music quickens during the bridge to the chorus, she removes the veil and tosses it to the floor. Sauntering downstage, she taunts and teases the bewildered yet cheering audience, becoming an amalgam of the innocence of popular sweetheart singer Debbie Boone and the raw sensuality of pop diva Tina Turner. "Never before," one reporter stated, "has a wedding dress looked more like a sleazy go-go outfit."[4] Shattering the myth of the chaste, virginal bride, Madonna touches herself and rolls around the stage bumping and grinding. Her new love, she sings, has made her feel "shiny and new."

Fast-forward to the summer of 2003. The 20th MTV Annual Video Music Awards open with a bridal backdrop complete with flowered archway and giant wedding cake. Two flower girls appear, attired in white dresses and studded Boy Toy belts. They walk across the stage strewing petals on the floor as in a wedding. Madonna fans recognize the two young girls as six-year old Lola (Lourdes) Maria Ciccone Leon, Madonna's eldest daughter, and Lola's friend, Honour.

A bride bursts out of the wedding cake. She lifts her veil to reveal—not Madonna—but pop sensation Britney Spears. Soon her darker, more carnal pop rival, Christina Aguilera, also dressed as a bride, joins her in a joint-rendition of "Like a Virgin." The homage continues as the bridal duo roll and writhe across the dance floor.

At the end of the song, Madonna herself materializes

Madonna's performance with Britney Spears (left) and Christina Aguilera (right) at the 2003 MTV Video Music Awards proved that, even after all these years, she is still a sex symbol capable of stirring up controversy.

from the cake. This time, she is dressed as a bridegroom, complete with top hat and tails. She dominates the stage, performing her single "Hollywood," from her *American Life* album. She further dominates the brides, who now function as her backup singers. Throughout the song, Madonna clutches Britney's waist and hips and strokes her face. In true wedding tradition, she provocatively removes the garter from Christina's thigh and throws it into the audience. Before the conclusion of the number, Madonna manages to French kiss both brides.

These lipstick kisses, especially the prolonged kiss between Madonna and Britney, caused nearly as much controversy as Madonna's first, attention-grabbing VMA appearance. Photos of the two locking lips appeared worldwide in tabloids and newspapers. An internet poll circulated entitled "The Kiss Heard 'Round the World." It asked for "Your take on the Big Kiss."[5]

The reaction of many was unsurprisingly negative. Some condemned Madonna and her younger protegees for female lechery while others singled out Madonna as ringleader, chastising her for exposing her daughter to "immoral" and "pornographic" behavior.

Shortly after the awards, Britney Spears insisted that the kiss was a harmless publicity stunt planned for and rehearsed ahead of time. "I didn't know it was going to be that long and everything," said Spears, who benefited from the kiss by shedding her previously squeaky-clean Mouseketeer image.[6] Years later, in 2006, Madonna publicly explained the meaning of the kiss to Lourdes, who was curious about her mother's sexual orientation, "I am the mommy pop star and she [Britney Spears] is the baby pop star. And I am kissing her to pass my energy on to her."[7]

Progressive Web sites at the time, however, read more into the performance. They viewed the skit as embracing lesbian sexuality and as a possible endorsement of gay marriage. One article concluded that, ". . . for Madonna (who has a twenty-year track record of actively challenging homophobia through her music) and Christina (who has also been very forthright in her support of gay rights), increasing lesbian visibility was likely to be at least some of the motivation."[8]

Chapter 2

What It Feels Like for a Girl

Madonna's live appearance in the 1984 MTV Video Music Awards was the first shocking moment in a career seemingly built on controversy. From her pointy bras to her public love life to her tell-all documentaries and banned videos, Madonna has consistently "caused a commotion," parodying sexual stereotypes such as the gold-digging blonde, the pregnant teen, the all-American cowgirl, and the hooker with the heart of gold. She seemingly condemns the patriarchal establishment that constructs these stereotypes—the straight male mind-set intent on retaining power status by categorizing women and other minorities into limited roles that devalue them. In a 2004 conversation about Madonna's celebrity, feminist Camille Paglia asserted, "I've often said I still haven't met that many women in my lifetime who have that compulsive drive toward egotistic assertion, that impulse for the grand gesture. It's mostly men who have that maniacal propulsion, though you can see it in people like Isadora Duncan and Martha Graham or Joan Crawford and Madonna—people who came from nothing and imposed their dreams on the world."[1]

What dream has Madonna imposed on the world? She embodies the conception of celebrity as an all-purpose entertainment package. "Music per se has never encompassed the full range of Madonna's aspirations," theorized journalist Jennifer Egan.

> "I never really planned to be an idol for millions of women all over the planet."

"[Her] contribution has been to usher in the phenomenon of star as multimedia impresario. . . . She's a creator of effects, of extravaganza, and she does this using imagery, sound, her voice, her body and anything else she can scare up."[2] Madonna belongs, Egan believes, in a classification of stars including Sean "Diddy" Combs and Martha Stewart, "defined less by any single talent or pursuit than by an array of projects and endeavors whose combined impact expands their personae exponentially."[3]

Social critics describe this phenomenon as "protean style." This is a reference to the Greek god Proteus and his ability to change shape to avoid capture. Contemporary "protean persons" use their chameleon-like adaptability to dominate social situations. They relate to people theatrically, assuming personas that audiences recognize as fiction. By doing so, real identities and motivations remain in question. What is conveyed are impressions, "of who and what I want you to believe I am."[4] Protean performers trade in charm or the vitality of their personalities, expecting their audience to react to them uncritically. Missing from this social equation is the give and take of reciprocal exchange, in which both parties respond to each other on equal terms. Instead, the protean person strives to "influence without being influenced in return."[5]

Characteristically, Madonna defines her creativity as inherently selfish, saying, "I don't think you can begin being creative by thinking how it's going to affect other people because that waters it down and ultimately a creative impulse has to come from a pure place."[6] Defending her many metamorphoses, she insists that change and variety is her means to liberate herself from the oppressive, male-dominated system, "What I did I did for myself, to free myself. I never really planned to be an idol for millions of women all over the planet."[7] She approaches projects, therefore, from personal rather than social motivation. "What am I going to get out of it? What am I going to learn from it? Is it going to challenge me? Is it going to take me to another place? Am I going to grow from it?" are some of the questions she asks herself.[8]

Her artistic decisions often appear to be a reaction to oppression. As one of her detractors suggests, "Madonna is not trying to rock the foundations of society. She's just angry about her Catholic upbringing, which encouraged repression of sexuality, and apparently she still is not over it. It's rather sad and immature that she needs to rebel for the sake of rebelling."[9]

Madonna, however, seems to consider herself less a rebel than a pioneer and a target for conservative fears. "Let's face it," she said, "all the stuff I've been going on about for years, people have learned to accept it. Nowadays, it doesn't sound so outrageous, that's how we are, every decade we become more open to ideas. Homosexuality is no longer a debate in pop culture, but even ten years ago it was considered terribly outrageous. We've come a long way."[10]

"Nowadays, it doesn't sound so outrageous . . ."

Madonna entered adolescence in the 1970s, at the height of the women's liberation movement, when women's issues were thrust into the political and social limelight. Liberal feminists, such as Germaine Greer and Gloria Steinem, vehemently encouraged women to challenge the prevailing social expectations of women. Madonna acknowledges their influence, "Our generation certainly has been encouraged to . . . be super-independent, get a great education, follow our dreams, kick ass, all that stuff." Yet, she refers to the reality of womanhood in the United States, with its different standards for men and women as a "bitter pill." These combined feelings of independence and vulnerability inspired Madonna to write the lyrics of "What It Feels Like For a Girl."[11]

In this song, Madonna speaks of the trade-off contemporary women face. A girl may possess intelligence and inner strength, and receive help cultivating these strengths, but be reluctant to demonstrate them, especially around male peers. Despite advances in gender equality, women commonly experience marginalization and misrepresentation in a society structured with a bias towards male ways of knowing. Vulnerability is still considered a desired feminine trait, and women continue to be referred to as the weaker sex.

The very anticipation of contradiction and controversy surrounding Madonna's work may be one of the keys to her lasting celebrity. "One thing that she's managed to do over the course of her career," maintains Madonna biographer J. Randy Taraborrelli, "has been to form what actually feels like a relationship with her public. By making moves that would be considered completely offensive to even her most die-hard fans, such as her *Sex* book, then coming back with wonderful moments of redemption, such as [her starring role in the movie musical] *Evita*, she's formed something that feels similar to what we all have with friends and family—moments of faith and forgiveness. Each well defined, each as real as the other, so that even those who aren't big fans of hers have a strong opinion about her."[12]

Meanwhile, her legacy has given direction to many young pop stars such as Britney Spears, who wrote about her in a 2004 issue of *Rolling Stone* magazine.

Though still the competition, endlessly proving that she can outlast and outsell each new wave of young performers, to them she is perceived as a benevolent godmother. "I would definitely not be here, doing what I'm doing, if it wasn't for Madonna," Spears reports. "I remember being eight or nine years old, running around my living room singing and dancing and wanting so much to be like her. Madonna's stage presence has inspired so many artists—you can see her influence in some of the younger generation like Kelly Clarkson and Shakira, who have picked up some of her moves. As part of the generation that's coming up, you look at Madonna and you don't want to let her down."[13]

Chapter 3

Mother and Father

"I wouldn't have turned out the way I was if I didn't have all those old-fashioned values to rebel against." —Madonna[1]

During her 1984 appearance on the live dance show *American Bandstand*, host Dick Clark asked Madonna what she planned to do when she grew up. Madonna's brash reply was "Mmmm, to rule the world."[2] Twenty-one years later, with sixteen albums, six world tours, twenty-two films, and six best-selling books to her credit, Madonna seems to have achieved this goal. Recipient of nearly a dozen "Best International Artist" awards, among countless accolades, she remains one of the richest, most prolific, and famous celebrities. Often referred to as the Queen of Pop, the *Guinness Book of World Records* sites Madonna as the most successful female recording artist of all time.

Yet Madonna's journey toward international stardom

represents a long, calculated effort. Her drive for achievement and recognition began in childhood. She entered the world on August 16, 1958, in Bay City, Michigan's Mercy Hospital as Madonna Louise Ciccone (chuh-KONE-ee), the eldest daughter and third child of Silvio Ciccone and Madonna Fortin. Learning and eventually rejecting her parents' conservative, Midwestern values helped to shape her independent spirit.

The youngest of six children in a first-generation Italian-American family, Silvio Ciccone was a devout Catholic with a strong work ethic, who strove to assimilate, or blend in with, American culture, moving away from his Italian roots in an attempt to get ahead. Of her father's family Madonna has said, "They weren't very educated, and I think in a way they represented an old lifestyle that my father really didn't want to have anything to do with. It's not that he was ashamed, really, but he wanted to be better."[3] Lyrics from the song "Easy Ride," on Madonna's *American Life* album, seem to echo her father's self-reliant attitude. They speak of wanting the "good life," the realization of the American Dream, but without a sense of entitlement— being owed it. The principal character of the song pulls him- or herself up by the bootstraps, rejecting the notion of an easy ride. Success and self-dignity belong to those willing to sacrifice the "blood and sweat" of hard work and perseverance to achieve goals.

Silvio adopted the nickname Tony; a name he

believed sounded less ethnic than Silvio. He became
the first in his family to attend college and to obtain
a white-collar job as an optic and defense engineer for
the Chrysler Corporation. A former sergeant in the Air
Force Reserve, he married Madonna Fortin, the sister of
military buddy Dale Fortin in 1955. Tony and Madonna
met at Dale Fortin's wedding in 1951. It seems to
have been a case of love at first sight for both of them.
Settling in the small town of Pontiac, Michigan, the
young couple had six children together: Anthony,
Martin, Madonna, Christopher, Paula, and Melanie.

Madonna's mother and namesake was an intelligent,
deeply religious woman with interests in dance, classical
music, and medicine. Unlike her husband, she hailed
from a successful, established, middle-class family
with an impressive pioneer pedigree.
Her French-Canadian ancestors were
noted for such resoluteness and
tenacity that, according to maternal
relative Claire Narbonne-Fortin,
"Nothing Madonna Junior does ever
surprises us."[4]

> **"Nothing Madonna Junior does ever surprises us."**

Friends of Madonna Senior agree that she was
a popular, fun-loving person who underplayed her
shrewdness and imagination in favor of traditional ideals
of femininity. Though she was not personally ambitious,
she admired this trait in others and was "very mature
for her age and very womanly and extremely dignified
for someone so young."[5] Madonna describes her mother
in terms of herself, "She was very beautiful. I look like

her. I have my father's eyes, but I have my mother's smile and a lot of her facial structure."[6]

Married life and full-time motherhood seemed to suit Madonna Senior, who may have aspired to the happy homemaker image exemplified by such popular icons as June Cleaver of the 1950s TV show *Leave it to Beaver*. Former neighbors confirm that Madonna Fortin Ciccone worked hard to fulfill both her wifely and motherly duties and to keep up her appearance for her husband. "She was the picture-perfect wife, waiting at the door, surrounded by her kids, who were bathed and clean for their good-night kiss with their dad," claims one of her friends.[7]

Her mother, Elsie Fortin, who initially objected to Madonna Senior's engagement to the son of an Italian immigrant, believed her daughter's marriage to Tony was a supportive and happy one. "My son-in-law was proud of the way my daughter looked and kept the house and children," she has stated. "They were always very warm and loving in front of the children."[8] Madonna's earliest memories corroborate this nurturing domestic portrait. In interviews she often refers to her mother as a playful and patient person, dancing and singing with her children to the radio and always picking up after everyone.

> **"I've got to push myself so hard because I have demons."**

Familial bliss, however, was relatively short-lived. In 1962, six months after the birth of her daughter

Melanie, Madonna Fortin Ciccone was diagnosed with breast cancer. Her employment as an X-ray technician during her courtship with Tony, before precautions were taken to limit exposure to radiation, may have directly contributed to her untimely death. Unwilling to wean her baby early, she postponed chemotherapy treatment. After a gradual decline and extensive hospitalization, she succumbed to cancer one year later at the age of thirty.

Madonna was five years old at the time of her mother's death. She attributes this event, and the realization of her own mortality, to the end of her childhood and the beginning of her drive to make a creative impact on the world. Madonna explained, "I've got to push myself so hard because I have demons. I won't live forever and when I die I don't want people to forget I existed."[9]

The trauma of losing her mother at such an early age has directly informed Madonna's work. *Truth or Dare*, the 1991 documentary of her ground-breaking "Blond Ambition" tour, featured a scene in which she and her younger brother Christopher visit the cemetery where their mother is buried. Madonna proceeds to lie down on top of the grave, while struggling to articulate her sense of loss. In a 1998 review of her *Ray of Light* album, a reporter wrote, "The third song in this personal trilogy is "Mer Girl," in which Madonna seems to be reconciling the death of her mother through the birth of her daughter [Lourdes]. 'I ran and I ran, I'm looking there still and I smelt her burning flesh, her rotting bones, her decay, I ran and I ran, I'm still running today,' she sings."[10]

Lyrics from the autobiographical song "Mother and Father," also featured in *American Life*, further reflect upon her mother's death. In this song, Madonna emphasizes the childhood perspective with repetitive, sing-song rhymes and vocals, reminiscent of schoolyard chants. As a young girl of five, she's aware of a lost connection. However the reality of her loss isn't clear to her. She copes with her mother's death through the self-comfort of crying, but doesn't understand why her mother isn't there to pacify her.

Chapter 4

Papa Don't Preach

My father was very strong. I don't agree with a lot of the ways he brought me up. I don't agree with a lot of his values, but he did have a lot of integrity.   —Madonna[1]

After her mother's death, Madonna's father buried his grief in the solace of a hectic work routine.[2] Madonna's immediate reaction was to withdraw into herself and her family, acting maternally toward her younger siblings and possessive of her father's attention. "Promise to Try," on the *Like A Prayer* album, addresses the vulnerability of that initial mourning period. It highlights the need of moving on without idealizing the past. Some reviewers believe it reveals the father/daughter relationship that existed in the aftermath of this personal tragedy, from Tony Ciccone's point of view.

The widowed Ciccone frequently enlisted his relatives to help him care for his children. This meant that Madonna and her siblings were sent to live with various relatives for extended periods of time. When they were together, housekeepers and babysitters were hired to supervise them while he worked. In 1966, three years after his wife's death, Tony Ciccone married Joan Gustafson, who reportedly fell in love not only with Tony but also with his children. At twenty-three, Joan was twelve years his junior—quite young to take on the challenge of mothering five small children and a baby. She had been their housekeeper for six months.

When asked to describe herself as an adolescent, Madonna has replied, "I see a very lonely girl who was searching for something, looking for a mother figure."[3] Yet Madonna has professed that she was unwilling to accept her father's second and current wife and to allow her to fulfill the role of mother for her. "My father made us all call her Mom," she said, but "I couldn't, I wouldn't say it."[4]

Madonna missed her real mother. She resented her stepmother's intrusion to the extent that her youthful mind dramatized their relationship as a Cinderella scenario. Joan Gustafson had been the only daughter in a relatively poor family. To establish dominance, she ran a strict, clean, and orderly home and expected her new family to pitch in with the housework as she had done as a child. Madonna told *TIME* magazine, "I was the oldest girl so I had a lot of adult responsibilities. I feel like all my adolescence was spent taking care of babies and changing diapers and baby-sitting. I have to say I resented it, because when all my friends were out playing, I felt like I had all these adult responsibilities. I think that's when I really thought about how I wanted to do something else and get away from all that. I really saw myself as the quintessential Cinderella."[5]

Following the arrival of two new siblings, Jennifer in 1967 and Mario in 1968, the now ten-member Ciccone family moved to a red brick, Colonial-style home in Rochester, Michigan, a suburb of Detroit. Rochester was idealized as ". . . a classic American suburban neighborhood—clean, crime-free, with large yards for the numerous neighborhood kids to play in."[6]

Yet this upscale, all-white neighborhood proved a repressive environment for the experimental, artistic souls of Madonna and her younger brother, Christopher. Christopher, a multitalented artist, has worked very closely with his sister throughout her career as a back-up dancer and a designer, directing her videos, developing sets for her concerts, and even accompanying her on her worldwide tours. He summarizes their reaction to Midwestern suburbia as follows: "Most of our aesthetic is rebellion against what we grew up with, American, or Colonial—I mean the 70s version of Colonial, the spindle-back chairs, the fake spinning wheel in the corner, the wooden icebox that held records."[7]

Madonna also traces her rebellious roots to this period of upheaval—the change of surroundings resulting from the move to Rochester coinciding with the emotional and physiological changes of puberty. She remembers being punished for her outspokenness, especially when questioning what she regarded as the "injustices of her religious upbringing." Rules enforced by her father and other authority figures prohibiting her from wearing pants to school like her brothers did, wearing makeup, chasing boys on the playground, or staying at home to pray in lieu of going to church each morning simply didn't make sense to her budding consciousness. She explained her motivation to assert her individuality amidst the Catholic discipline as follows: "When you go to Catholic school, you have to wear uniforms, and everything is decided for you. Since you have no choice but to wear your uniform, you go out of your way to do things that are different in order to stand out."[8]

In 1989, Madonna jokingly boasted to an *Interview* magazine reporter, "Probably about the same time as I began to rebel against the church and my family, my breasts started to grow. I went through puberty before most of the girls in my class."[9] Puberty brought with it an interest in boys and sexuality. Despite rumors, her behavior toward the opposite sex ultimately manifested itself as forward and flirtatious rather than promiscuous. Though she played the part of a vamp, it was just a façade. She was not the kind of girl who ended up in the backseat of a car. According to her grandmother, Elsie Fortin, ". . . it just seemed so obvious that Madonna was letting off steam. Her stepmother and father were too strict with the kids back home."[10]

Madonna admitted in 1991, "Because I was a really aggressive woman, guys thought of me as a really strange girl. I know I frightened them. I didn't add up for them."[11] Her reputation as a wild child was fueled

Despite her controversial work, Madonna and her father still have a good relationship. They even shared a few laughs when Tony joined Madonna on the Arsenio Hall Show in 1992.

by a tendency toward exhibitionism. During a parochial school talent show, for example, ten-year-old Madonna danced suggestively with a bikini costume and florescent body paint to The Who's song "Baba O'Riley," which refers to a "teenage wasteland." The glowing painted flowers highlighted the near-nakedness of her body as she twirled under a black light. In the finale of a junior high talent show, she flashed the audience. After performing to the song "Secret Agent Man," she revealed that all she wore under her oversized trench coat was a dance leotard.

Her dance routines outraged her parents and her teachers despite the ovations she received from fellow classmates. Madonna, who attended Catholic schools until high school, later defended her schoolgirl provocation, insisting "the talent show was my one night a year to show them who I really was and what I could really be, and I just wanted to do totally outrageous stuff."[12] These audacious pubescent shenanigans prefigure her later video-oriented career. In fact, each night of her first tour, aptly named the Virgin Tour, ended with a nod to the effects of her stage presence on parental authority. When the concert played hometown Detroit, she convinced her father to come out onstage and literally escort her off. At other engagements, a taped voice-over of a stern male voice ordered her offstage, to which she coyly replied, "Daddy, do I hafta?"[13]

Chapter 5

Causing a Commotion

If my father hadn't been so strict I wouldn't be
who I am today.   —Madonna[1]

As Madonna got older, her home life became
increasingly competitive; an aspect that her father
encouraged with rewards for achievements such as good
grades. She vied for her father's attention, and felt like
an outsider in her own home. Chores and schoolwork
dominated her life and that of her siblings. A typical
summertime routine for the Ciccone children was,
Madonna states:

> I had to work in my father's vegetable garden
> every summer. My father has a work ethic that
> makes mine look nonexistent, so the school's-out-
> for-summer stuff does not exist in my family.
> Basically, I was either put to work at my house,
> weeding and spraying insecticide, or we had to go
> to my grandparents' house in Pennsylvania, where
> we'd fix up the house and the yard all summer.[2]

Her brothers reacted to this strict, goal-oriented upbringing by escaping into psychedelic music and drugs. Madonna said that her big brothers, especially her oldest brother Anthony, influenced her life in interesting ways by introducing her to vegetarianism and books of an alternative or "subversive" nature, such as those written by Charles Bukowski and Richard Brautigan. "You know," she said, "they were into the whole LSD drug culture, Maharishi orchestra. I was really frightened by them but completely enamored of them as well. And they've both lived very adventurous lives."[3]

Madonna's desire for attention, parental and otherwise, led her instead on a path toward artistic experimentation. "I wasn't rebellious in a conventional way," she has explained about her high school years. "I cared about being good at something. I didn't shave under my arms and I didn't wear makeup. But I studied hard and got good grades."[4] Though her father seems to have imposed his achievement goals on the entire family, no one pushed Madonna harder than herself. She juggled an active social life, including various boyfriends, with a busy after-school routine. Madonna took classes in piano and jazz dance, and participated in cheerleading, French club, and choir. She also helped to found the Rochester Adams High School Thespian Society, performing lead roles in productions of the *Addams Family*, *My Fair Lady*, *The Wizard of Oz*, and

Cheerleading was one of the many after-school activities that Madonna participated in while at Rochester Adams High School. This photo was taken during her freshman year.

Cinderella. "Every time there was a talent show or a musical at school, I was always in it," she said.[5]

For one such Thespian Society event, she spent weeks rehearsing a song-and-dance routine. She developed the song "Turn Back, O Man," from the musical *Godspell*, into a solo number. *Godspell* was written in 1971 as a contemporary take on the Passion of Christ and his relationship with his disciples. This fun, flirtatious song opens the second act, allowing sassy character Sonia, an urban Mary Magdalen, to toy interactively with the audience. It was originally written for Sonia Manzano, later "Maria" on the children's television show *Sesame Street*. According to composer Stephen Schwarz, the real-life Sonia had a kind of Mae Westian naughty/naive quality to her character. Nick Twomey, a school sweetheart, concedes that it was a perfect vehicle for Madonna's similar personality. Twomey states, "It was a breakout event for Madonna. She pretty much seduced the entire gymnasium, myself and the teachers included. It wasn't wildly erotic, but Madonna was Madonna even back then, and she knew how to work the crowd."[6]

Chapter 6

You Can Dance, for Inspiration

I always had the idea that I wanted to be a performer, but I wasn't sure if I wanted to sing or dance or be an actress or what, so I concentrated on dancing.　　　—Madonna[1]

Madonna's high school drama teacher, Beverly Gibson, believed her to be a popular student with great charisma and a strong stage presence. However, Madonna professed that she struggled to fit in with her peers until she found her niche in ballet. "When I was in the tenth grade I knew a girl who was a serious ballet dancer. She looked really smarter than your average girl but in an interesting, offbeat way. So I attached myself to her and she brought me to a ballet class, and that's where I met Christopher Flynn, who saved me from my high school turmoil."[2]

Some Madonna devotees tout Christopher Flynn as "arguably the first Madonna-positive person."[3] Lyrics from "In This Life" on Madonna's *Erotica* album attempt to explain his lasting influence on her. Madonna refers to Flynn as a loving father figure that taught her to respect herself. She also communicates the belief that people should not be judged by their sexual orientation.

Flynn, a middle-aged former ballet dancer, ran the Rochester School of Ballet. He had studied under Vladimir "the Duke" Dokoudovsky, a student of George Balanchine among other famous choreographers, who approached dance as theatre. The Duke taught for thirty years at Ballet Arts, one of the oldest continuously operating dance schools in New York City.[4] By working with the Duke at Ballet Arts, Flynn followed in the footsteps of silver screen notables Agnes DeMille, Leslie Caron, and Jose Ferrer. They contributed their talents to movie musicals such as *Oklahoma!*, *State Fair*, and *Gigi*.

During his brief dance career, Flynn performed in the prestigious Joffrey Ballet Company. His was a professional dance studio, and most of his pupils had been trained in ballet from an early age. Although Madonna had taken a variety of dance classes, she came to him a virtual novice. She had to work very hard to match the abilities of the group.

Ballet quickly became a lifestyle for Madonna. The self-discipline necessary for growth as a dancer transformed her personality from a wise-cracking show-off to an introspective, somewhat aloof nonconformist. Becoming more comfortable with her body through dance may have helped her to develop confidence and

As high school progressed, Madonna became more engrossed in ballet and more comfortable with her body. Less concerned with conformity, Madonna wore funky clothes and cut her hair short, as shown in this photo taken during her junior year.

ease with herself and her own sense of style. She cut her hair short and wore clothes that clashed, such as overalls and bold-printed shirts with combat boots. Remarking on her high school appearance, friend Lisa Gaggino remembers, "She wasn't afraid to be different, and at that age it's hard to be different without worrying what other people think of you."[5] Madonna later explained her style, "Where is it written that in order to be a better dancer you have to wear a black leotard and pink tights and have your hair in a bun?"[6]

Madonna no longer vied to be the center of attention in class and among friends. This change became most apparent to others at the beginning of her senior year when she spent most of her free time practicing dance and hanging out with her dance teacher and fellow ballet students. According to high school friends, "It was a major flip-flop. People were thinking: 'What is it with her?'"[7]

Dance was a gateway for discovery in other arts in which she has maintained a lifelong interest—painting, poetry, literature, and music. Impressed with Madonna's youthful talent and ambition, Flynn took it upon himself to become her mentor, exposing her to Detroit's museums, operas, concerts, art galleries, and fashion shows. At home she read teen magazines such as *Seventeen* and *Glamour* and listened to popular bands such as the Monkees, or Motown artists like Stevie Wonder, Marvin Gaye, and the Jackson 5. With Flynn she discussed poetry, books, and art. One of Flynn's

friends explains that Chris, "knew without ever
meeting her family that Madonna lacked any cultural or
intellectual background and yet he was certain that all
she needed was someone to take her under his wing."[8]

Flynn was the first artistic person Madonna knew.
He encouraged her to broaden her tastes to include
classical music, Pre-Raphaelite painters, and poets such
as Sylvia Plath and Anne Sexton. "My sister and I used
to read all of her [Anne Sexton's] poems when we were
in high school because she looked like our mother,"
Madonna said. "She talks about death a lot and breast
cancer and mothers, all these death images that we were
obsessed with."[9]

Flynn also was the first person to introduce Madonna
to a homosexual lifestyle. Madonna reveals that until
she met Flynn she saw herself only through macho
heterosexual eyes. "I didn't understand the concept of
gay at that time," she insists. "All I knew was that my
ballet teacher was different from everybody else. He was
so alive. He had a certain theatricality about him. He
made you proud of yourself, just the way he came up
to me and put my face in his hand and said, 'You are
beautiful.' . . . I fell in love with him and the way he
treated me."[10]

Detroit has a long-standing history as a significant
gay metropolis. Since the 1940s, nightclubs and bars
have been central to Detroit's gay world. Madonna
felt accepted around Flynn and his friends. When she
accompanied Flynn to discotheques such as Menjo's

(still a thriving gay gathering place) she felt free to cut loose and dance uninhibitedly. Regarding her teenage exploration of gay subculture, Madonna has said, "In school and in my neighborhood and everything, I felt like such an outsider, a misfit, a weirdo. And suddenly when I went to the gay club, I didn't feel that way anymore. I just felt at home. I had a whole new sense of myself."[11]

It is not surprising that her entrée into gay culture was so enlightening. When Madonna's brother Christopher began taking ballet lessons, Flynn was quick to point out to Madonna that Christopher was gay. Flynn was likewise a confidante for her own bisexual experimentation. Madonna's first long-term sexual relationship was of a lesbian nature. Kathy, the serious ballet student who first introduced her to Flynn's ballet class, became her lover at the age of fifteen. Though not an exclusive relationship, their affair supposedly lasted through high school and into their early twenties.[12]

Chapter 7

You'll See

Christopher Flynn undoubtedly paved the way for Madonna to leave Rochester Hills to pursue her dance dreams. In 1976, he accepted a visiting professorship in the dance program at the University of Michigan, Ann Arbor. At the same time, he convinced Madonna to graduate a semester early from Rochester Adams High School and to apply for a scholarship through the University of Michigan Music Department so that she could continue to study under him. Certainly his influence must have helped her to win a full four-year dance scholarship to this institution. However, Madonna's own intelligence and talent proved equally instrumental in propelling her forward. Ever an achiever, she ranked high academically in her class and tested at an IQ of 140 (the average IQ is 100). Her high school teachers wrote glowing recommendations to the scholarship committee, praising her motivation and creativity.

Madonna has admitted that her father would have "freaked out" if he had known of the intensity of her relationship with Flynn and of their frequent forays to gay nightclubs. Though pleased by her scholarship, the practical Tony Ciccone held reservations about dance as a career. Madonna said about her father, "He's a sensible guy, and what's dancing to him? He can't imagine that you can make a living from it or work at it or be proud of it or think of it as an accomplishment. He could never really be supportive of it."[1] From this point onward, Madonna carefully constructed her own support network. Her parents, it seems, had no direct impact on the future direction of her life.

Once at Ann Arbor, Madonna committed herself to a demanding dance schedule. She was a focused student, always on time for dance classes. Dance faculty such as Professor Gay Delanghe considered her a credit to the college. When she allowed herself to have fun, Madonna went out dancing with Flynn or other students. One night she and her friends wandered into a bar called The Blue Frogge. There she flirted with a handsome waiter named Stephen Bray, a drummer in a local band. Briefly they were lovers, but their friendship would endure many future musical collaborations.

In February of 1977, Madonna spent a weekend in New York City auditioning for a six-week summer workshop at the Alvin Ailey American Dance Theatre. She won the scholarship and once her spring semester at the University of Michigan concluded, she traveled again to the Big Apple for a summer apprenticeship in an Ailey student company directed by Kelvin Rotardier. Founded in 1958 by African-American dancer/choreographer Alvin Ailey, the Ailey Dance Theatre blends classical, jazz, modern, and African-American movement traditions. Ailey's mission was to break color and ethnic barriers by providing a multi-racial dance environment.

At that time, Ailey's company had its headquarters in the American Dance Center on East Fifty-ninth Street between Second and Third Avenue. They shared a building with the school and company of Pearl Lang, formerly a soloist for the legendary Martha Graham. Once used as a settlement house, the space had a gritty, bustling, lived-in feel. Walls depicting dancing figures painted by student artists enlivened the décor of barres and mirrors. Lang and her dancers occupied the ground floor while Ailey's group rehearsed in the upper floors.

"He could never really be supportive of it."

According to Jennifer Dunning's biography, *Alvin Ailey: A Life in Dance*, hundreds of young New Yorkers and would-be dancers from around the country converged on the school. Everyone seemed to pass through, from actors, musicians, and dance stars to reviewers for whom a short-lived series of classes was arranged.[2] Madonna acknowledges the exhilaration and intimidation of that summer school experience. "Everyone was Hispanic or black," she said, "and everyone wanted to be a star."[3]

Coincidentally, when Madonna returned to the University of Michigan for her sophomore year, Pearl Lang surfaced in the dance program as an artist-in-residence. Although she did not yet take classes with her, Madonna danced in a recital of a new work Lang created for the program. Lang and Madonna were destined to meet up again that summer at the American Dance Festival (ADF) held that year at Duke University in Durham, North Carolina.

By this time, Madonna was impatient to train with a professional dance company. Her mentor, Christopher Flynn, agreed that she was ready for this challenge and once again encouraged her to make a move toward her goals. The prevailing myth, a myth Madonna helped to perpetuate in her 1983 interview in *Star Hits* magazine shortly after her first album debut, professes that Madonna arrived in New York City in the summer of 1978 with only $35 and a lot of ambition.

Madonna auditioned for the intensive, six-week summer workshops.

It was a gutsy decision to abandon her degree, her scholarship, which was her meal ticket, the sheltered University of Michigan campus close to home, and supportive friends like Flynn. However, Madonna did not take this risk unprepared. College friends, such as Linda Alaniz, concur that she worked nights and weekends during her sophomore year to amass a substantial nest egg. Arriving in New York she settled with friends at Columbia University rather than wandering aimlessly near Times Square to be in "the center of everything."[4]

Madonna did not, in fact, spend much time in New York City that summer. Instead, she headed south to Duke University for the American Dance Festival (ADF). This was ADF's first season in North Carolina. Begun in 1934, at Bennington College in Vermont, as an experimental dance laboratory for modern-dance pioneers Martha Graham, Hanya Holm, Doris Humphrey, and Charles Weidman, the festival is committed to encouraging, supporting, and preserving America's modern-dance heritage.

Along with hundreds of prospective students from around the country, Madonna auditioned for the intensive, six-week summer workshops. Pearl Lang, as guest faculty choreographer, awarded Madonna one of the twenty available scholarships. Madonna therefore spent the summer in West Durham attending Lang's advanced modern-dance technique and repertory classes in a white-framed building nicknamed the Ark because of its narrow, two-person entryway. Madonna has been touted as "perhaps the most famous person to ever sleep on [Duke University's] East Campus."[5] At the end of the festival, Madonna approached Lang for a position in her New York company. Lang agreed to extend her a provisional placement that fall.

Chapter 8

Gambler

Pearl Lang decisively asserts herself as Madonna's primary ballet and modern-dance mentor, subsequent to her university training. She considered Madonna to be a beautiful performer with "the most gorgeous back."[1] This is high praise coming from the premier Martha Graham protégé. Graham's revolutionary dance technique arose from her exploration of the potential greatness of the body and her observations of breathing. She developed principles of contraction and release in order to mimic what she perceived as the nervous, sharp, and zigzag energy of modern life. Although the center of the body is key for creating her characteristically jagged, twisted dance images with earthbound, slashing momentum, in Graham's philosophy the impulse of all movement stems from a dancer's back. Madonna was not destined to meet and study with Martha Graham until long after she became famous.

Madonna's relationship with Lang, however, was far less idealistic and awestruck. Lang vividly recalls her reunion with Madonna in New York after the summer workshop at Duke University. In a 1994 issue of the newspaper *The Forward*, she explains, ". . . we were reviving my work, 'I Never Saw Another Butterfly,' based on the children's poems and drawings from the Terezin/Theresienstadt concentration camp and four weeks after I began rehearsals in New York, the door opened and Madonna appeared. She was thin and wistful looking, sad and lost, but she was very talented. She appeared in the second cast at both the 92nd Street Y [in 1978] and [when] Joseph Papp produced it at the Public Theater in 1979."[2]

Madonna, however, seems never to have gotten used to the daily routine and Spartan demands of Lang's choreography. Lang looked out for Madonna, using her personal connections to find her employment as a coat-check girl at the Russian Tearoom next to Carnegie Hall to help pay for her expenses. She also invited her to parties at her apartment. Passions ran high between them, however. A dancer describes the two squaring off before the company. "It was like watching two tigresses prowling around, sizing each other up," the dancer commented.[3]

Madonna herself is very thrifty in her assessment of Lang. Ironically, she has remarked that Lang, who is Jewish, employed an approach to dance that was "painful, dark, and guilt-ridden. Very Catholic."[4] Madonna felt stifled in the fiercely competitive atmosphere of the professional New York dance circuit, where progress within a company is often slow and uncertain. The original movie and TV-series *Fame*, for which Madonna auditioned in 1979, immortalizes the artistic struggle of that time from the point of view of young actors, musicians, and dancers. It may have paralleled Madonna's experiences in Lang's company. Episodes of *Fame* were fictionalized accounts of life in a professional training school, patterned after New York's High School of the Performing Arts. Just as Lang's artistic vision reigned supreme in her company, the school's demanding but compassionate dance teacher, portrayed by Debbie Allen, who headed the cast in both the film and the series, was very similar.

Yet it is clear that after touring with Lang, Madonna did not believe that she would find fame as a dancer in Lang's company or any other. After a year of juggling dance rehearsals and performances with menial dead-end jobs, such as a cashier at a Dunkin' Donuts and stints as an artist and photography model, Madonna was ready to move on. Whatever her reasoning, Madonna eventually confronted Lang, announcing that she was going to become a rock singer instead of a dancer. "With all that promise she gave up dancing," Lang succinctly sums up her reaction to Madonna. "The problem with her from the beginning," Lang continues, "was that she was never willing to see a discipline through to the end, at least one like dance that took enormous stamina."[5]

Chapter 9

Born to Be Alive

Maybe if she had never come to Paris, Madonna
would have continued taking dance lessons,
going to auditions, and never even tried to make
it as a singer!

—Patrick Hernandez[1]

Under Lang's tutelage, Madonna inhabited a
sophisticated social circle that included fine art lovers
and New York intellectuals. Meanwhile, worlds apart
from this artistic environment, pop culture from the
mid-1970s through the early 1980s underwent a disco
dance craze. Disco is short for discotheque—the French
word for nightclub, particularly those that featured
recorded music rather than live bands. Whereas
the music of the late 1960s and early 1970s was
dominated by groups that emerged from the folk-rock
movement, including Simon and Garfunkel, the Mamas
and the Papas, and show bands like Jefferson Airplane

and The Who, disco took its roots from funk and soul music. Its up-tempo, "four to the floor" bass line catered to the intimate sphere of the dance club rather than to a massive concert crowd.

Recording stars such as Gloria Gaynor, Donna Summer, and Van McCoy released hit disco songs in 1975 such as "Never Can Say Goodbye," "Love to Love You Baby," and the "Hustle." But the film *Saturday Night Fever* propelled disco into the mainstream in 1977. *Saturday Night Fever* showcased disco music, disco dancing, and nightclub culture. It starred John Travolta as Tony Manero, a Brooklyn youth contending with harsh social realities. For the character Tony, and the many young people he was modeled after, disco dancing served as a means of release and escape.

"There was a real need for music that people could dance to," Gloria Gaynor once said. "The world needed an inexpensive way to release the tension and frustration of a very prominent economic struggle that was coming. Disco music was common ground for people of every age group, or every nationality and every creed and color."[2]

Disco was indeed a worldwide phenomenon, as exemplified by the career of Patrick Hernandez. Often panned by critics as a one-hit wonder, unlike many disco artists he did write and compose most of his material. Though a veteran musician in his native France, Hernandez rocketed to international stardom with his 1978 disco hit, "Born to Be Alive." By 1979, his album of the same name received fifty-two gold and platinum awards from over fifty different countries. A remix of his hit single by Columbia Records became number one in disco charts and reached the Top 40 across the United States.

Hernandez's producer, Jean Van Lieu, his wife Muriel, and partner Jean-Claude Pellerin held open auditions in New York in the spring of 1979 for a worldwide tour. They were seeking interesting personalities, a mixed gender and racial group to serve as backup dancers and singers for their star performer. They planned a variety show around Hernandez, similar to a cabaret act.

> "We saw right away that she had more punch than the others."

Madonna stood out among the fifteen hundred hopefuls who attended this open audition. After three days of auditions in which they had to convince a reluctant Madonna to sing for them, they decided to bring her to Paris and groom her as a star rather than a chorus girl. "We saw right away that she had more punch than the others," Hernandez said. "Instead of selecting her to dance like an idiot behind me, we separated her from the other performers. We wanted to bring her to France so she could record."[3]

Despite her announcement to Lang about becoming a rock singer, Madonna still identified herself as a dancer. Utilizing Hernandez's connections, she envisioned herself becoming a dancer/actress. Once in Paris and under contract with the Van Lieus and Pellerin, her

room, board, and expenses were fully paid for. She
had plenty of free time to explore the city. Her Parisian
patrons also indulged her demands for dance lessons.
However, they intended to develop and market
Madonna as another disco singer, and they knew this
transformation would take time. They had allowed
Hernandez, a skilled musician long under their employ,
to hone his talent for nearly a year before recording
his first single. To their minds, Madonna, a complete
unknown, needed more polishing. They arranged for
her to receive music, singing, and conversational French
lessons. Slowly they introduced her
to European society, making sure to
photograph her alongside Hernandez.
They even commissioned someone
to compose a song for her, entitled
"She's a Real Disco Queen."

> **She was eager to focus all of her energies on furthering her own career.**

Madonna grew deeply dissatisfied
with the pace of her career as
dictated by her managers. Cultural and personality
differences worked against their relationship. Madonna's
disciplined work ethic clashed with their laid-back
management style. She was simply not a high priority
for Pellerin and the Van Lieus. Although Madonna
enjoyed access to the luxurious lifestyle of an international
star, she had no desire to bask in Hernandez's shadow.
She was eager to focus all of her energies on furthering
her own career.

Furthermore, Madonna did not respond well to the
disco music that they wanted her to sing. At the time,

she preferred the punk sound of singers such as Debbie Harry of Blondie or Chrissie Hynde of the Pretenders. In retrospect, Hernandez finds her resentment of disco ironic. "Funny," he has said, "when she became a success years later, it was by singing the kinds of pop dance tunes we were trying to get her to record in the first place. In the end, her music was not at all avant-garde."[4]

Hernandez believes that his fame motivated Madonna and that ultimately he proved to be a lasting influence on her life direction. He and his friends succeeded in convincing her that she could likewise become a major recording star. However, she was prepared to take her chances back in the United States. After six months with Hernandez and his troupe in Paris, she returned to New York City. There, she would soon hit the streets with something new to occupy her mind.

Chapter 10

Madonna in the Sky

Weeks before leaving for Paris with Hernandez, Madonna encountered the Gilroy brothers. She met Dan Gilroy and his brother Ed at a party thrown by Norris Burroughs, a graffiti artist and mutual friend. Dan and Ed lived in a renovated synagogue in Corona, the Italian section of Queens. Though both had day jobs, they performed regularly together as the musical comedy act Bil and Gil. Dan and Madonna quickly became an item and kept up a long-distance flirtation once she left for Europe. All during her stay in Paris, Dan sent her funny postcards, drawings, and song lyrics.

When Madonna returned from Europe, she moved in with the Gilroys. Twelve years her senior, Dan Gilroy seized the baton from Christopher Flynn as life-changing creative male mentor—though in music instead of dance. For nearly a year, Dan Gilroy supported Madonna and furthered her music education. He encouraged her in her songwriting pursuits and taught her how to play the guitar and drums, which he believed would showcase her energy and rhythmic abilities. Madonna continued dancing, but now practiced on drums and guitar just as fervently. An avid diarist, then and now, she also began to use material she wrote in her journals as the basis for song lyrics. Her first attempts at songwriting are perceived as an important self-revelation. "I don't know where they came from," she is quoted as saying. "It was like magic. I'd write a song every day. I said: 'Wow, I was meant to do this.'"[1]

Ed Gilroy credits his brother as a nurturing muse for her writing process. He explains that her first songs were self-indulgent, yet therapeutic, dealing with "loss, low self-esteem, things that had been inside her for who knows how long. She had stability here [in the Gilroy's studio], security here, a positive environment to reach back into those times and try and express herself."[2]

Dan, as singer/songwriter, and Ed, as lead guitarist, headed a punk rock garage band named the Breakfast Club. As Madonna's musical talent emerged, she became their drummer, with her dancer friend Angie Smit on bass. It was an amateur musical act, but Madonna pushed for perfection. She eventually took on the role of band manager, organizing paying gigs for them in local night clubs that booked young punk and pre-punk hard rock bands, such as Country Bluegrass Blues (CBGBs), the UK Club, and Bo's Space. Though the entire band dressed in signature white, and Madonna occasionally belched loudly between songs to get attention, Angie most often stole the show with her see-through tops and leggy, dancer's body.

In 1980, Angie Smit left the band. She couldn't commit to the demanding rehearsal schedule, and her musical skills didn't advance along with the others. Former Breakfast Club member Gary Burke took over as bassist, with Mike Monahan on drums. Madonna switched to keyboard and frequently shared vocals with the Gilroys, singing duets and solo numbers. The new members contributed to a tighter sound that attracted the attention of club owners. Yet with Angie gone, Madonna was eager to front the band herself and to secure a record deal. The Gilroys, however, were unwilling to allow her to assert herself as lead vocalist or to favor her material to the exclusion of theirs. By summer 1980, Madonna decided it was time to move on. She explains her decision to end her relationship with the Gilroys: "They weren't as interested in the commercial end as I was. It never occurred to me to get into this business and *not* be a huge success."[3]

> "It never occurred to me to get into this business and *not* be a huge success."

Though Burke remained Breakfast Club's bassist, he and Monahan, who was infatuated with Madonna, agreed to back her. They formed the short-lived trio, Madonna and the Sky. The trio rehearsed in the Music Building, located in a seedy area of West Thirty-ninth. After a brief romance with Madonna, Monahan parted with the band. Stephen Bray, Madonna's former Michigan boyfriend, moved to New York to replace him. Along with Burke and Madonna, he helped to form the band Emmy (also known as the Millionaires). Though Bray's talent and ambition matched Madonna's, it took nearly a year for the band to establish a foothold in the New York club scene.

Away from the relative safety and luxury of the Gilroys and their synagogue studio, Madonna faced tough times. She lived in squalid conditions, sometimes without the means to pay for heat, and accepted cast-off clothing and makeup from friends. Impatience and desperation nearly drove her to return to the family home in Michigan. Ironically, Madonna admits nostalgia for her pre-star past, "To me, recording this album [*Confessions on a Dance Floor*, 2005] was like going back. It was so liberating. I want to be in the s*** holes. I want to be in a small place with no furniture. I want to keep it the way it was when I started, sitting on the floor and scribbling in my notebook. I work best under those circumstances."[4]

Chapter 11

Right on Track

Madonna received her big break in the spring of 1981 when Emmy performed at the popular nightspot Max's Kansas City. At the time, Adam Alter and Camille Barbone headed Gotham Sound Studios, a recording studio located in the Music Building, where Emmy rehearsed. Madonna managed to persuade Alter to listen to a tape of Emmy songs. Alter, whose father was a jazz instrumentalist and composer, financed the Gotham partnership. He convinced Barbone, who performed most of the management duties at Gotham, to scout Madonna during their show. "I didn't realize that this really interesting young woman that I kept running into and exchanging one liners with was the same artist that my partner was hounding me to listen to," Barbone recalls.[1] Impressed with Madonna but not with what she described as her "lousy band,"[2] Barbone agreed to manage Madonna as a solo performer. At the same time, the management at Max's, owners of an independent record label, offered Emmy a recording contract.

After years of struggle, Madonna received two attractive contract offers in one night. Perhaps predictably, Madonna chose the option that thrust her alone in the spotlight. One of Barbone's first maneuvers as Madonna's business manager was to fire Bray, Burke, and fellow Emmy band mate Brian Syms. She arranged for Alter to finance an apartment for their new discovery along with a weekly stipend and access to the Gotham recording studio. Additionally, she found Madonna part-time employment as a house cleaner, allowing her to earn a steady income between photo shoots, industry appearances, performances, and recording sessions with professional musicians.

Barbone would later rehire Stephen Bray as Madonna's backup drummer. His collaboration with Madonna was destined to outlast Barbone. Barbone became too emotionally involved with the young singer to manage her effectively. Aside from the sexual tension that existed between Madonna and her female manager, they disagreed about musical direction. Barbone and Alter were primarily interested in rock and roll whereas Madonna began to embrace disco. In a 1984 *Rolling Stone* magazine article, "Madonna Goes All the Way," Stephen Bray recalls with a sigh that under management Madonna "was playing really raucous rock & roll, really influenced by the Pretenders and the Police. She used to really belt."[3]

Madonna walked out on her contract with Gotham Sound in February 1982. It took three years for Barbone to settle this breach and move on. She contended Madonna was stolen away from her. "After doing a lot of work on Madonna, building a band of top notch, now well-known, musicians, doing a four-song master. . . spending a great deal of money on salaries, Madonna's overhead, networking and generally managing Madonna smack into the middle of mainstream music, the word got out. People began to contact her directly and promise her things that I couldn't deliver. My company was brand new, terribly under-funded, and I wasn't a member of the good old boy network of managers and labels that work hand and hand," she said.[4]

In the meantime, Bray and Burke reformed the Breakfast Club with the Gilroys. Eventually, in 1987, long after Madonna had launched a successful career, the Breakfast Club debuted their first and only self-titled album on the Ze Record label. For the album, Bray and Dan Gilroy co-wrote "Right on Track," which became a Top Ten hit. Though they were not written with Madonna in mind, the lyrics of this song seem appropriate in light of Madonna's relationships with Bray, Gilroy, and Barbone as her stardom became imminent. They hint at the type of maneuvering that leaves others in the dust.[5]

Chapter 12

Everybody, Everybody

She's—she's, you know, Madonna! . . . She
really works you to the bone.
                    —Debi Mazar on Madonna[1]

Going to clubs in the early 1980s seemed to be the
best way to hear and experience the latest dance music.
Nightclubs are meant to function as laboratories of style
where new trends and modes of being are spearheaded.[2]
After hanging out at various dance clubs, carefully
observing and absorbing the dancing she liked best,
Madonna developed her own choreographed music.
Analyzing the New York club scene, she and Stephen
Bray realized that funky dance records were in style
on the radio and on the dance floor. They wrote and
recorded a demo tape with four dance tracks, including
"Burning Up," "Everybody," and "Ain't No Big Deal."
Their lyrics encouraged getting into the groove of
dancing and singing. Madonna describes her music as

"the kind that helps people to forget about the problems of the world. It's just to cheer people up," she says. "People go out to dance to get away and forget about their problems like a holiday and that's what the music's about—to get together and forget."[3]

Once again a free agent, but now with contacts and exposure—compliments of Gotham Sound—Madonna did her own legwork to promote her demo, systematically touring night clubs and discos to meet music business professionals. Simon Frith concludes that "Madonna hit New York at exactly the right club moment. The city's dance music was in the midst of its glorious ride along the cusp of the mechanical and the soulful, when R&B [rhythm and blues] conventions of vocal dirt and desire were being deployed by a new generation of engineers who layered the dance floor's background noise with a percussive care, a sense of temporal order that turned even the most sweaty workout into an intellectual exercise."[4]

> **"I'd spend all night on the dance floor in some hideous outfit while all the pretty, skinny, fashionable girls threw their drinks on me."**

Madonna's ambition to be on the receiving end of this communal desire led her to the Manhattan nightclub Danceteria. Danceteria was the place to be seen—a celebrity hangout then considered one of the hippest venues in New York. Now a hotel, it had three floors for dancing, live shows, and lounging. Madonna said, "'Don't You Want Me,' by the Human League, reminds me of the days of Danceteria in New York. I lived on the Lower East Side, at Fourth and B, in a tenement apartment—without air conditioning. I didn't have a record deal yet, but my demos were off the press, and I used to go to Danceteria every weekend, trying to meet the DJ or an A&R [artist and repertoire] person to give my tape to. I'd spend all night on the dance floor in some hideous outfit while all the pretty, skinny, fashionable girls threw their drinks on me. But when that song came on, I forgot my humiliation. I didn't care that I was soaking wet and didn't have any friends."[5]

Yet Madonna was far from friendless, and she had a flair for fashion that upstaged all those other "pretty, skinny girls." She often went club hopping with actress Debi Mazar, fashion retailer Maripol, dancer Erica Bell, and artist Fred Brathwaite (Fab Five Freddy), among other young artists and trendsetters. Vito Bruno, a club manager, stated, "Madonna and her friends were the kinds of kids you wanted in your venue. She was a standout—trendy and eye-catching. They got into the VIP rooms before they were VIP's."[6]

In fact, Madonna seemed to be in her element on the dance floor. She created her own style of dance and dress. She wore layered thrift store finds with lots of accessories—leggings, miniskirts or baggy pants tied with ribbons, cropped denim jackets, hair bows or leather caps, mesh tank tops, lingerie used as outerwear, fingerless gloves, rubber bracelets, crucifix earrings and necklaces. Her dance moves were both suggestive and aggressive, with pelvic grinds that showed off her bare midriff, sexy twirls punctuated by flirty head tosses, and hands raised to frame her face or to run her hands through her dyed, tousled locks. Madonna describes the attitude that she exemplified:

> What went on at American clubs or raves was perfect but temporary democracies of desire, an ideal world where racial, sexual and social divisions were dissolved in the communal abandon of the dance floor. The mass euphoria and emotional solidarity I experienced while dancing at downtown clubs seemed like a possible model for a future society.[7]

Eventually, her persistence paid off. At Danceteria, she met DJ Mark Kamins, who had contacts with several industry professionals and had just started his own music company. Kamins was also an A & R scout for the independent Island Records, which represented pop acts such as U2. Kamins recalls the day he first gave her songs a spin. "Madonna was a regular at the Danceteria. She had great style and had to be the center of attraction. She always hung out in the booth, one day she gave me a demo to play—it worked. At that time I was working with the Talking Heads so I knew the people at Sire Records. I played them the demo and they gave me a single deal. I produced "Everybody" and it went to #1 in the dance charts. The rest is history."[8]

Chapter 13

Starlight, Star Bright

Sire Records, distributed by Warner Brothers Music, initially plugged Madonna as a black artist. To Sire executives, her soulful dance sound seemed more hip hop than punk or pop. They deliberately masked her racial identity to capture a growing market of R & B listeners who might assume from her urban style that she was black. Unimpressed with "Ain't No Big Deal," the A side of the 1982 recording that Kamins produced, Sire Records representative Michael Rosenblatt placed the song "Everybody" on both sides of the 12-inch vinyl record. The cover of the Everybody single featured an urban street collage with skyscrapers, traffic lights, tenements, graffiti, sidewalks, and fire hydrants. Except for what appears to be a white police officer, everyone else in the collage is African American, including the central figure of a young boy on roller skates trailing a colorful bouquet of helium balloons. Madonna is not represented.

Racial ambiguity aside, Sire's strategy mirrored what Madonna had been doing all along—promoting her singing and dancing abilities in the nightclubs. They favored a slow introduction, producing a string of one-song albums that would first receive club exposure and then radio airtime. Following the success of "Everybody," they released the singles "Burning Up/Physical Attraction," "Lucky Star," and "Holiday" in 1983. These songs were compiled on her first Sire album, *Madonna*, which also debuted in 1983.

John "Jellybean" Benitez produced the latter song, "Holiday." In 1981, Benitez became the resident DJ of the Fun House, a Manhattan club frequented by aspiring rap and hip-hop artists such as LL Cool J, Run DMC, and Lisa Lisa. Known for its carnival atmosphere, with the dance party lasting on weekends from ten at night until ten in the morning, the Fun House featured an enormous clown face. Benitez spun records from inside its cavernous, gaping mouth.

For three years at the Fun House, Benitez influenced musical trends. He pioneered Latin Freestyle, a fusion of disco and break dance music with Latin American rhythms and syncopated drums. His production work for artists such as Madonna led to more studio projects including film work and the formation of two record labels— H.O.L.A. (Home of Latino Artists) Recordings, which releases bilingual tracks, and Jellybean Recordings.

According to Benitez,

> At that point, clubs had a much stronger influence on what was being played on the radio, and that

helped to change what you call Top 40. I mean you would have all different kinds of people, but it was really a place where kids went to dance and sweat, and they'd stay at their spot on the dance floor for three or four hours. But it wasn't like they were dancing to one song. It was like a train. Some people would get on, stop, continue, but most people were there for the whole trek.[1]

Madonna made frequent stops at the Fun House, and began a tempestuous two-year relationship with Benitez in 1983 as both of their careers flourished. He and Madonna seemed to their mutual friends to be truly in love and soon became engaged. They made a great team and helped each other through the trauma of budding celebrity. A shrewd and ambitious businessman, Benitez, and his publicist, showed Madonna how to manipulate the media and to exploit her position in the industry.

Perhaps as a result of Benitez's guidance, Madonna took control promoting her career. Each Friday she joined Sire promoter Bobby Shaw and club DJs for business meetings in his office, where they discussed music business news and sampled fresh releases. She also secured a high-powered manager, Freddy DeMann of Weisner-DeMann Entertainment, who had worked for Michael Jackson. Her association with DeMann would be a long and lucrative one, lasting several decades. DeMann immediately sought to market Madonna to a mass audience through the fledgling medium of music videos.

Chapter 14

Keep on Pushin' Me

"Yes, she used me to network into the business,"
he later recalled. "But I did the same to her."
—Jellybean Benitez on Madonna[1]

Academic Pamela Robertson touts music videos as
representing "the post-modern explosion of technologies,
acceleration of images and information, and mass-media
access."[2] Robertson views Madonna as "the ultimate
postmodern video star," comfortable with image,
representation, and artifice as features of music
production. In other words, she takes full advantage of
the latest technology on tour and in the recording studio
to enhance her music and image. She rarely appears
unplugged/acoustic.

Certainly music videos allowed Madonna to merge
her dance training with her musical abilities. She already
had two music videos under her belt before Freddy
DeMann added clout and capital to her video

phenomenon by commissioning the pop classic
Borderline, directed by Mary Lambert. Madonna's first
video, *Everybody*, was a low-budget, promotional affair
primarily focusing on disco dancing. In it, a close-
cropped boyish-looking Madonna sways and sings in
a nightclub setting backed by her brother Christopher
and Erica Bell who would later reprise their dancer roles
for her *Lucky Star* video. Her second video, *Burning
Up*, used freeze frames to create a somewhat surreal,
disjointed montage of sexual imagery—eyes, chains,
smoke, and lasers. The opening sequence suggests a
nighttime encounter. Madonna, a Greek goddess
come to life, writhes and sings in the middle of a dark,
desolate road while her boyfriend drives toward her.
At the end of the video, she takes his place in the
driver's seat.

Borderline has a more straightforward story line,
one that may have mimicked her on again, off again
romance with Jellybean Benitez. A streetwise Madonna,
discovered by a fashion photographer while break
dancing, leaves her friends and Latino boyfriend
behind. Though the street sequences are shot in color,
Madonna's dalliances with the photographer are shown
in dreamlike black and white. Eventually, however,
Madonna becomes bored with this elegance and is
kicked out of the photographer's studio. She returns to
her colorful street life to win back her boyfriend.

DeMann correctly believed that pop songs such as
"Borderline," supported by professional videos, held the

potential for the more mainstream appeal he wanted for Madonna. For Madonna, the transition from live musical performance to film seemed natural. This was not so for many musicians who had established themselves before video and believed music to be more important than imagery. In an MTV News segment covering a New Music Seminar panel held in New York in 1984, Madonna defends the music video format amidst the criticism of those in the panel who believed that videos detracted from the music. "I'm sorry," she said, "but kids today worship the television, so I think it's a great way to reach them."[3] When John Oates of Hall and Oates countered that he resented the necessity of being an actor as well as a musician in videos, Madonna quipped, "Yeah but, but listen. When you perform on-stage you're acting. I mean that's the performance. I mean if someone puts a camera on you what's the difference?"[4]

> **"I've been in touch with that aspect of my personality since I was five."**

Later that year Madonna attempted to explain her ease in front of the camera in the article "Madonna Goes All the Way" for *Rolling Stone* magazine. Writer Christopher Connelly asks the question: How did she manage to put across such seething sexuality where so many [recording artists] have tried and failed? Madonna replies, "I think that has to do with them not being in touch with that aspect of their personality. They say,

'Well, I have to do a video now, and a pop star has to come on sexually, so how do I do that?' instead of being in touch with that part of their self to begin with. I've been in touch with that aspect of my personality since I was five."[5]

Chapter 15

Burning Up

Sire delayed the release of her next album, *Like a Virgin*, until November 1984 to boost their profit margin on *Madonna*, which after a slow start was selling in the millions. For *Like A Virgin*, which she playfully dedicated to the virgins of the world, Madonna had her pick of producers. She decided upon Nile Rodgers, who had successfully engineered records for such diverse artists as Diana Ross, David Bowie, Duran Duran, and INXS. "I chose to work with Nile Rodgers," she told MTV News, "because I think that he's a genius and I wanted to work with a genius on my record."[1]

A skilled musician, Rodgers may also have been chosen for his expertise in arranging songs. Madonna's musical ear was primarily instinctual. She had never received significant formal music training and did not know music terminology. For most of the songs on the album, she collaborated with Stephen Bray. Bray describes their songwriting process, "I've always kind of made the rib cage and the skeleton [music] of the song already—she's there for the last things like the eyebrows and the haircut [lyrics]. She writes in a stream of mood really."[2]

Madonna later corroborated her habit of getting into a certain mood and writing from that mood. In 1989, she admitted that in her first albums she was primarily interested in coming across as "entertaining and charming and frivolous and sweet."[3] At the time of that interview, her sixth album, *Like A Prayer*, had just been released. Unlike her other albums, she recorded *Like A Prayer* in the studio with live musicians, rather than overdubbing the vocals on top of the finished music. Although her approach to recording her music had evolved—and continued to do so as her 1998 electronic album, *Ray of Light*, which alternated between minimalist production and modern studio effects, would contest—Madonna's method of developing songs had not changed since her first releases. It remained a team or group effort. She further explained,

> "She writes in a stream of mood really."

Sometimes the music is sort of there, already written by either Pat Leonard [an arranger/producer] or Stephen Bray. They give it to me and it inspires or insinuates a lyric or feeling. Then I write out the words in a free form, and we change the music to fit the form. Other times I'll start out with lyrics, or I'll have written a poem and I'll want to put that to music. Then I end up changing the words a little bit to make them more musical.

Sometimes I'll hear the melody in my head. I don't
write music and I don't read music, so I'll go
to Pat Leonard, who is an extremely talented
musician, and I'll sing it to him and make him play
it, making chords out of it. Then I write the words
to the song.[4]

The success of her first albums and videos opened
up many other opportunities for Madonna. In 1983
DeMann arranged for her involvement in the movie
Vision Quest, in which she has a cameo as a nightclub
singer, resulting in the videos "Crazy for You" and
"Gambler." This experience led to the title role in the
upbeat screwball comedy *Desperately Seeking Susan*,
which was set in New York City.

Madonna believed that acting in feature films was
just an extension of the work she was already doing
in music videos and onstage performances. "When you
are a dancer," she explained to MTV in 1984, "you can
only perform with your body and I think that I had a
lot of things to say in other ways besides movement, so
that's why I got into the music business. And to me film
is just the ultimate. It's just the embodiment of it all.
You can do all of it. I mean it's captured forever on
celluloid."[5]

Although intended to be a star vehicle for actress
Rosanna Arquette, director Susan Seidelman expanded
Madonna's role in *Desperately Seeking Susan* on the
strength of her unforgettable comedic characterization
of the street-wise Susan. The plot involves a bored
housewife Roberta [Arquette] who becomes obsessed

with an adventurer named Susan [Madonna] she encounters in the personal ads of a newspaper. After adopting Susan's manner of dress, Roberta has an accident and gets amnesia. She then believes she's Susan and the mistaken identity leads to mayhem.

Taking advantage of Madonna's rising popularity, Seidelman filmed an extensive nightclub sequence in Madonna's old haunt the Danceteria, showcasing her song "Into the Groove," which became a successful follow-up single. Many critics therefore hailed *Desperately Seeking Susan* as "Madonna's Movie." Initially, this upset Arquette, who had not anticipated being upstaged by a showbiz newcomer. However, reviewers such as Roger Ebert showed no favoritism between the two young stars. "[The film] has its moments," he wrote in a March 1985 review, "and many of them involve the different kinds of special appeal that Arquette and Madonna are able to generate. They are very particular individuals, and in a dizzying plot they somehow succeed in creating specific, interesting characters."[6]

> **"You can do all of it. I mean it's captured forever on celluloid."**

Madonna's finesse in this role seemed to come as no surprise to her manager Freddy DeMann. He believed that the part was made for her. Though she later appeared in over a dozen movies, she was destined to "desperately seek" another film role that suited her abilities for over a decade. Arguably, her documentary

Truth or Dare, in which she played herself, and her portrayal of the cartoon gangster's moll Breathless Mahoney in the film *Dick Tracy*, are exceptions. But not until her characterization of Evita Peron in the 1996 movie musical *Evita* would Madonna again receive such rave reviews for her feature film work.

Chapter 16

Why's It So Hard

By 1985, Madonna was an international celebrity.
The critical and commercial success of her albums,
videos, and films prompted even a non-industry news
source such as *TIME* magazine to feature her on its
cover. Fame had its downside. Ironically, for a take-
charge "Material Girl," juggling her financial rewards
seemed stressful. In her video for this number one
single, Madonna wittily parodies the gold-digging
attributes of sex symbol Marilyn Monroe. Wearing
a dress copied from the Marilyn Monroe hit film
Gentlemen Prefer Blondes, in which Monroe announces
that diamonds are a girl's best friend, Madonna's video
persona longs for men with cold, hard cash.

Feminist theorists such as Sonya Andermahr
embraced Madonna's self-reliance, claiming that
"Madonna calls her own shots . . . [S]he exercises more
power and control over the production, marketing and
financial value of her image than any female icon before

her."[1] Yet, an interview with MTV News around this time captures her angst,

> Well now that I am successful I have a million more things to worry about. Before I was just basically interested in my survival like what I was going to eat and what I was going to wear when it got cold outside and where I was going to live. But now I have to worry about who is ripping me off and is my accountant paying all of my bills and is my lawyer making all of those deals for me and um, you know, boring and mundane things like that. Things I don't want to worry about and I have to invest my money or I'm going to be taxed and you know, I have to find a place and I have to do this and I have to do that. And I have to pay everyone and I have to hire someone to make sure that everyone is doing all of those things and ughhhh!![2]

Her love life also seems to have been strained. Early in the year she broke off her engagement with Jellybean Benitez, who was willing to start a family with her. Benitez's friend Arthur Baker commented of the breakup that, "I knew he [Benitez] was really into her . . . But she was the one in charge. She's a diva—man, they like to command attention. All singers are like that."[3]

In 1985, Madonna was still empire building, branching out in as many directions as her talent and ambition would take her to prove her versatility beyond recording artist. A full-scale, nationwide concert tour, "The Virgin Tour," immediately sold out in twenty-eight major cities. Appearances in charity concerts such as Live-Aid, which benefited AIDS awareness, were

In addition to her tour schedule, Madonna performed at charity concerts like the Live-Aid famine relief concert in Philadelphia during her whirlwind summer of 1985.

planned. She would not allow for the fever pitch of her career to accommodate motherhood until the birth of her daughter Lourdes, a full decade later. However, by the end of the summer, Madonna would marry into a Hollywood family.

Mr. Right turned out to be actor/director Sean Penn. Son of television director Leo Penn and actress Eileen Ryan, in the mid-1980s Penn established himself as one of the most talented and rebellious stars of his generation, cast as intense hot-shots in popular teen movies such as *Taps*, *Fast Times at Ridgemont High*, and *The Falcon and the Snowman*. In a 2005 interview for Britain's *Now* magazine he remarked, "I wouldn't comfortably call myself a rebel, but there is a certain necessary level of dissatisfaction that's, as it turns out, important, because to be complacent is creatively criminal. It's a constant struggle to find your own voice and to be loyal to it. There's only a price to be paid for not doing that, as far as I can tell."[4]

Penn and Madonna met on the set of the *Material Girl* video through their mutual matchmaking friends, Mary Lambert and James Foley, who would later direct Madonna in the comedy *Who's That Girl?* and in several videos from her *True Blue* album, including *Live to Tell* and *Papa Don't Preach*. In many ways their pairing represented a culture clash of East versus West. Whereas Madonna enjoyed glamour, fashion, and an urbane social life, she described Penn as a "cowboy poet," a rugged, outdoorsy individualist interested in boating, hunting, and shooting. Hard drinking, chain smoking, brooding, short-tempered . . . in contrast, Madonna's upbeat, life-affirming persona held none of these somewhat self-destructive tendencies. Furthermore, the straightforward Penn had little patience for the spirited antics and sexual ambiguity of Madonna's East Coast friends. Yet what he did share with them was a passion for art and the courage to take creative risks.

The fact that their whirlwind romance coincided with the rapid upswing in Madonna's popularity contributed to its undoing. Though not yet the icon that she is today, the media had already begun to consider her public property, with intrusive candid photographers or "paparazzi" constantly on hand to photograph her every movement. It was difficult to travel in any youth circle in 1985 without seeing evidence of her mass appeal. For example, Madonna kicked off her first concert tour at the Paramount Theatre that May in Seattle, Washington, selecting the rap group the Beastie Boys as her opening act. Teenage fans, dubbed "Madonna wannabe's," flocked to this and subsequent concerts, dressed to look like her. A performance review in *Rolling Stone* magazine claimed that "at least 80 percent of the girls in the crowd had [tried] their [hardest] to mimic their idol's looks, from bleaching and tousling their hair to wearing such Madonna-associated items as see-through blouses, finger-less gloves, and crucifix earrings."[5]

The video *Dress You Up*, featuring live footage of the

Madonna's marriage to Sean Penn was marred by constant media scrutiny.

Detroit leg of her "Virgin Tour," captures this fan phenomenon. Its long opening sequence focuses on excited fans happily entering the concert venue. As the music begins, Madonna, clad in a loud green and purple mini skirt ensemble with a multi-colored paisley jacket, shimmies down a white staircase, enthusiastically prancing toward a sea of audience clones dressed nearly as flamboyantly as she is. "I thought it was amazing," Madonna remarked in hindsight, "amazing that a certain way I chose to look and dress became an obsession. Certainly it was not what I set out to do. I think those things just happen by chance. I don't think you can set out to do something like that. But I thought it was really flattering."[6]

At the end of each show, thousands of balloons, each printed with the phrase "Dreams Can Come True," cascaded upon the audience, released from nets that held them aloft above the stage. The conclusion of the videotape *Madonna Live: the Virgin Tour*, released in 1991, explains this Disney-esque finale. As lights and music fade, Madonna triumphantly intones, "I went to New York. I had a dream. I wanted to be a big star. I didn't know anybody. I wanted to dance. I wanted to sing. I wanted to do all those things. I wanted to make people happy. I wanted to be famous. I wanted everybody to love me. I wanted to be a star. I worked really hard and my dream came true."[7]

Chapter 17

Poison Penns

Sean said to me once, "You know, I made a
mistake, I mistook a great first date for a
marriage. I should have just taken her out."
                    —Eileen Ryan Penn on Madonna[1]

Living his personal life under the persistent media
blitz generated by his relationship with Madonna was
not a dream come true for the privacy-loving Penn.
Nevertheless, in July 1985, Penn proposed to Madonna
in Nashville, the location of his movie *At Close Range*.
They set a wedding date of August 16, Madonna's
twenty-seventh birthday. By all accounts, the ceremony
was a nightmare. In stark contrast to her later marriage
to Guy Ritchie in 2000, for which she successfully hired
security to keep the media and all other uninvited guests
away, the paparazzi invaded their Malibu wedding.

Precautions had been made to keep the location of
their nuptials secret. Sean Penn's friend and personal

assistant, Meegan Ochs, personally phoned everyone in the wedding party the day before with directions to the beachfront property of developer Kurt Unger, a friend of the Penn family.[2] However, someone informed the press, and photographers and cameramen surrounded the home. Some even tried to infiltrate it. Reportedly, the groom became so frustrated that he baited the press helicopters that flew overhead, scrawling an obscenity in the sand so the paparazzi couldn't print any photos. Also, he fired warning shots at them using one of the many guns in his collection. Even Madonna, who typically welcomed such fanfare, displayed her annoyance by giving the finger to the camera while Penn stuck his head up her dress.[3] The press had already dubbed the pair the "Poison Penns" because of Penn's periodically violent reaction to tabloid activity. Undeterred, reporters held their ground, and helicopter noise compromised the audibility of the ceremony.

Tension among the guests also marred the day. There was a sharp division between old money and new, the Hollywood crowd (including Cher, Tom Cruise, Diane Keaton, Rosanna Arquette, Christopher Walken, and the Sheen Family) mixing uneasily with the New York contingent (including Andy Warhol, Erica Bell, Keith Haring, and Debi Mazar). Sibling rivalry added to the chaos. Maid of Honor Paula Ciccone, Madonna's look-alike younger sister, threw a tantrum at the reception proclaiming, "This should have been my wedding day, not hers . . . All this attention should have been mine."[4]

Madonna later likened the experience to a Busby
Berkeley musical because of the whirlwind of activity
and personalities generating theatrics on many levels.
"I think back on it now . . . ," remembered director
James Foley, ". . . and that wedding was a kind of
specific white heat of whatever 'celebrity' was in
the middle of the eighties, bearing down with this
unflinching hot light. But it's like when you're shooting
and sometimes the actor will complain, 'Does that light
have to be so close?' And that light was such a pressure
on Sean and Madonna."[5]

Penn, though widely thought of as the best actor of
his generation, seemed to hit rock bottom during his
four-year marriage to Madonna. He teamed up with her
in the ill-received comedy *Shanghai Surprise* and in a
limited run of David Rabe's stage play *Goose and Tom-
Tom*, to mixed reviews. While distinguishing himself
as a murderer in *At Close Range* and a hotheaded cop
in *Colors*, these extreme characters underscored the
violence in his own life. His most publicized role became
that of bodyguard husband, aggressively shielding
his wife from the paparazzi. Headlines chronicled his
reckless driving, assault charges, and verbal abuse of
Madonna and her friends. In 1987 he served a month-
long sentence in an L.A. County jail after repeatedly
violating probation. Madonna likewise pressed domestic
assault charges against him but dropped them after
filing for divorce in 1989.

In one interview given shortly before their divorce

was finalized, Madonna expressed more sadness than regret about the demise of their marriage, describing her relationship with Penn as "two fires rubbing up against each other." She claimed that there was no one single breaking point that led to divorce. "I have great respect for him," she said. "It's like most relationships that fail. It's not one thing, it's many things that go on over a period of time."[6] Penn has since confessed that he behaved like an angry, headstrong young man confronting a lot of inner demons. In his opinion, their differing attitudes toward fame and artistic integrity strained their union. "I never liked being under the spotlight," he said. "Our marriage guaranteed that we lived in the public gaze, which meant that we had no real marriage at all. We didn't even have time to have a proper conversation. She was in the process of becoming the biggest star in the world. I just wanted to make my films and hide."[7]

Despite marital difficulties, Madonna's career continued to flourish. She remained focused and prolific, co-producing her *True Blue* album in 1986, which she dedicated to her husband's "very pure vision of love" by naming it after one of his favorite expressions.[8] *True Blue* garnered serious attention from music critics who believed it was a turning point in her career that signaled "her transition from pop star to pop artist."[9] Critic Robert Hilburn remarked of the album that "Madonna visualizes music so that her best work seems equally designed with the stage or screen in mind—not

Madonna reveals yet another new look at the 1987 premiere of her film *Who's That Girl?*

just the jukebox."[10] This is particularly true of "Papa Don't Preach," which tackles the issue of teenage pregnancy. Its video featured Madonna as an unwed mother-to-be stalwartly deciding to keep her baby. This character does not contradict her pro-choice leanings. In fact, in her next concert she used the song to criticize male authority figures such as the pope and Ronald Reagan, who opposed birth control and tried to legislate against a woman's control over her own body. Along with the sensitive subject matter came a new look—a short, tomboyish hairdo that softened her appearance, and a firmer, athletic figure.

In 1987 she released *Who's That Girl?*, her first soundtrack album, named for her latest film and her first worldwide concert tour. Her second tour was noticeably more polished and theatrical than her first. There had never before been "a more imaginative or forceful showcase for the feminine sensibility in pop."[11]

"Madonna is simply the first female entertainer who has ever starred in a show of this scope," wrote Mikal Gilmore. He described her ninety-minute tour-de-force as "a fusion of Broadway style choreography and post-disco song and dance that tops the standards set by previous live concert firebrands like Prince and Michael Jackson."[12]

Madonna's career was definitely on a roll. "She doesn't rest," noted *Who's That Girl?* costar Coati Mundi speaking about her frantic work ethic. "She's got a bit of that perfectionist thing in her. She was doing the

Madonna observed first-hand the worldwide scope of her stardom when she had to be escorted through London's Heathrow airport during her first-ever tour in Britain in 1987.

movie, and the soundtrack album for the movie, and also planning her "Who's That Girl?" tour at the same time. She's doing all this stuff, plus she's got the lead in the film!"[13] Just as Penn's artistry received a boost after their divorce (he would soon star in a succession of powerful movies including *Casualties of War* and *State of Grace*) Madonna's next album, *Like A Prayer*, became widely recognized as one of her most mature and accomplished offerings.

Chapter 18

I Can Feel Your Power

People are asleep, and you've got to do what you can to wake them up.   —Madonna[1]

Many critics, biographers, academics, and reviewers alike, view the accomplishment of her *Like A Prayer* album as the zenith of Madonna's career. *Like A Prayer* was perceived as an ambitious, confessional record covering universal themes, in which "Madonna is brutally frank about the dissolution of her marriage, her ambivalence toward her father and even her feelings of loss about her mother."[2]

Madonna seemed to feel that the time was right to reveal a darker, more spiritual side of her nature quite apart from the slick, glamorous, manufactured image normally presented to the public. "I didn't try to candy coat anything or make it more palatable for mass consumption, I guess," she said. "I wrote what I felt."[3]

Throughout the album, she lays bare her feelings

about her relationships with family and loved ones. Songs like "Till Death Do Us Part," convey the sense that Madonna used the album as a form of therapy, working through the trauma of her broken marriage in order to move on with her life. Conflicted feelings and loyalties crop up in this song. People you love and who love you can hurt you the most. We push each other away in spite of ourselves.

She hints at the positive aspects of this exercise in self-examination. "The overall emotional context of the album is drawn from what I was going through when I was growing up," she explained, "and I'm still growing up."[4]

> **"The idea is to somehow bring it down to a level that everyone can relate to."**

Tension between the sacred and the profane, especially as explored in the video for her title hit, ultimately pulled focus away from the more blatantly self-revelatory songs in the album. Flirtation with religious iconography, including puns on her name, had been a part of Madonna's image since she first appeared on the music scene. Indeed she has admitted to consciously appropriating religious symbols such as crucifixes and rosaries, wearing them and toying with them, in order to demystify them or "Take these iconographic symbols that are held away from everybody in glass cases and say, Here is another way of looking at it. . . The idea is to somehow bring it down to a level that everyone can relate to."[5]

Her motivation also has been to connect spirituality with sexuality. Though Christianity places them in conflict with each other, she sees this separation as detrimental to relationships. "That's why everyone has affairs and they cheat on their wives or their husbands," she said. "People separate things. They have someone they idolize, and then they idolize them so much that they put them on a pedestal and see them as so virginal and holy that they can't have fun with them. And then they have to find people to have fun with and get low-down and dirty. They don't let the id in themselves come out, know what I mean? I think you have to put the two together with people."[6]

Coming to terms with her childhood while developing this album meant coming to terms with the Catholic faith in which she was raised. "We went to church all the time. We went to Sunday school, we went to catechism, and during Lent we went to church every day. Our sense of art, drama, and decadence all came from this. So did our sense of the power of secrets that lie in all the dark corners. All of that came from church," Madonna said.[7]

In the Catholic Church, the Madonna is the Virgin Mary, the mother of God or Jesus. Catholics view Jesus' virgin birth as a literal birth by a virginal woman. However, the concept of virgin birth, also termed second birth, occurs in most of the mythologies of the world. According to scholar Joseph Campbell, a virgin birth is a metaphor for spiritual transformation. It is a reference to a spiritual event rather than an historical one. Instead of childbirth, an enlightened mind-set has been attained. "Until that comes," he says, "you have only a human animal not a human being."[8]

Madonna's *Like A Prayer* video centers on transformation. Although just a few minutes long, it has an extremely complex plot, resembling that of a murder melodrama. The following account by Madonna explains how the video was conceived:

> Originally when I recorded the song I would play it over and over again, trying to get a visual sense of what sort of story or fantasy it evoked in me. I kept imagining this story about a girl who was madly in love with a black man, set in the South, with this forbidden interracial love affair. And the guy she's in love with sings in a choir. So she's obsessed with him and goes to church all of the time. And then it turned into a bigger story, which was about racism and bigotry.[9]

Once Mary Lambert became involved as director of the project, the story line changed dramatically. She expanded the scope of the plot and incorporated esoteric Roman Catholic references such as stigmata (marks or sores corresponding to the wounds of Jesus) and *ecce homo* (bleeding associated with Christ's crown of thorns). Her instincts in the suspense and horror film genre, having directed Stephen King's *Pet Sematary*, evidence themselves in the quick action cuts, strobelike dream sequences, and credible special effects.

The video's synopsis reads as follows:

> A girl on the street witnesses an assault on a

young woman. Afraid to get involved because she might get hurt, she is frozen in fear. A black man walking down the street also sees the incident and decides to help the woman. But just then, the police arrive and arrest him. As they take him away, she looks up and sees one of the gang members who assaulted the girl. He gives her a look that says she'll be dead if she tells. The girl runs, not knowing where to go, until she sees a church. She goes in and sees a saint in a cage who looks very much like the black man on the street, and says a prayer to help her make the right decision. He seems to be crying but she is not sure. She lies down on a pew and falls into a dream in which she begins to tumble in space with no one to break her fall. Suddenly she is caught by a woman who represents earth and emotional strength and who tosses her back up and tells her to do the right thing. Still dreaming, she returns to the saint and her religious and erotic feelings begin to stir. The saint becomes a man. She picks up a knife and cuts her hand. That's the guilt in Catholicism that if you do something that feels good you will be punished. As the choir sings, she reaches an orgasmic crescendo of sexual fulfillment intertwined with her love of God. She knows that nothing's going to happen to her if she does what she believes is right. She wakes up, goes to the jail, tells the police the man is innocent, and he is freed.[10]

The result is evocative of medieval passion plays, a tradition of religious theatrical performance in the church. The theatrics are made explicit. At the end of the video the performers bow, and a curtain closes.

Perhaps coincidentally, when the video was made, Madonna had just finished performing in a Broadway play, *Speed the Plow* by David Mamet. She had also negotiated a $5 million sponsorship deal with the Pepsi-Cola Company for a commercial featuring the same song. Even though the commercial and the video had vastly different themes, fundamentalist Christian groups, such as the American Family Association and Roman Catholic organizations in Italy, confused the two. They protested the video proclaiming it blasphemous and offensive to believers. They also threatened to boycott Pepsi-Cola products. Confronted by this pressure, Pepsi canceled all ads featuring Madonna.

Madonna studies became something of a fad on college campuses.

If religious factions and corporate America took exception to the work, academia found it exceptional. Several academics analyzed the video and wrote lengthy essays about it along with other singles from the album. Madonna studies became something of a fad on college campuses. In 1992, for example, classes using Madonna works as text spanned English, Women's Studies, Contemporary Culture, and Musicology curriculum. Songs and videos from the *Like A Prayer* album alone were studied at Rutgers, Harvard, and the University of California. Camille Paglia, professor of Humanities at University of the Arts in Philadelphia, maintained, "It is absolutely legitimate to show [in a course] how images of the present inherit the meanings of the past."[11] She concluded that with the video *Like A Prayer*, "Madonna has made a major contribution to the history of women. She has rejoined and healed the split halves of woman: Mary, the Blessed Virgin and holy mother, and Mary Magdalene, the harlot."[12]

Chapter 19

Live Out Your Fantasies Here With Me

Capitalizing on the publicity generated by the *Like a Prayer* album, in 1990 Madonna mounted a provocative new worldwide tour, "Blond Ambition." By now seasoned at touring, she wanted to break all the rules in terms of content and execution. "The biggest thing we tried to do is change the shape of concerts," choreographer Vincent Patterson is quoted as saying. "Instead of just presenting songs, we wanted to combine fashion, Broadway, rock and the performance arts."[1] Striving for worldwide domination, the tour opened in Japan and closed in France, playing twenty-seven cities in three continents in just over four months. She and her brother Christopher, serving as artistic director, demanded state-of-the-art technology. Over a hundred crewmembers were needed to assemble the 80 x 70-foot stage, which took eighteen trucks to haul around. The centerpiece was a hydraulic platform, which Madonna descended at the beginning of the show, singing her crotch-grabbing anthem of empowerment and self-respect "Express Yourself." For the number, a recreation of her futuristic MTV video, Madonna donned a tailored suit and monocle. Underneath she revealed industrial armor of another nature—a stunning cone-shaped bustier designed by Jean-Paul Gaultier.

Madonna was not the only one who wore lingerie during the show. Two female vocalists, Niki Haris and Donna DeLory, accompanied her throughout the performance along with seven male dancers. In some numbers the men danced suggestively with each other. In one, they wore bullet bras. When asked if her fan base was sophisticated enough to digest this progressive sexual statement, Madonna replied, "They digest it on a lot of different levels. Some people will see it and be disgusted by it, but maybe they'll be unconsciously aroused by it, maybe they'll be unconsciously challenged by the idea of men in women's lingerie. Then there are people who see it and are amused by it, see the irony of it, see things that maybe frightened them before and know that it's not something to be so frightened of. If people keep seeing it and seeing it and seeing it, eventually it's not going to be such a strange thing."[2]

Madonna had based her *Express Yourself* video on Fritz Lang's sci-fi classic, *Metropolis*, about the loss of individuality in mass society. *Metropolis* takes place in 2026; a future marked by separate though deeply intertwined societal divisions; the haves and the have-nots—the thinker/planners and the worker/ achievers. A mediator eventually emerges, bridging the gap between the two. Madonna may have undertaken this role during her tour. She book-ended "Blond Ambition," alternately loud and lewd, introspective, coy, and upbeat, with a similar message of interdependence. Spanning an impressive eighteen songs, her concert juxtaposed the social and family drama of "Like a Prayer" and "Oh Father," with a feverish, masturbatory rendition of "Like a Virgin." It concluded with the mantra of "Keep It Together."

Not everyone was willing to embrace this mix of self-assertion, sexual freedom, and interrelationships. Officials in Toronto threatened to arrest Madonna if she didn't change the show. She refused, but they didn't press charges. When the Vatican spoke out against the show weeks prior to her Italian tour dates, Madonna rallied. Proud of her Italian heritage and always willing to advertise it, she staged a press conference defending her artistic vision. "My show is a theatrical presentation of my music," she told reporters. "Like theatre, it asks questions, promotes thought, and takes you on an emotional journey. I don't endorse a way of life but I describe one. The audience is left to make its own decisions and judgements. That's what I consider freedom of speech, expression, and thought."[3]

Her tour coincided with the release of her album *I'm Breathless*, linked to the Warren Beatty movie *Dick Tracy*; a stylized, action-comedy based on Chester

Gould's 1930s detective comic strip. In the movie, Madonna plays bad-girl love interest Breathless Mahoney, a sexy nightclub singer and gangster's moll. Broadway composer Stephen Sondheim wrote three show tunes for her Breathless character, the style of which forms the basis for the rest of the torch songs in the album. Their urbane lyrics and intricate compositions represented a departure for Madonna, yet she proved she was capable of handling the musical theatre genre. Her confident renditions foreshadow the virtuosity she would later display in the filmed version of the opera *Evita*.

"Vogue" appeared in both the new tour and the new album. The only disco tune in *I'm Breathless*, the song refers to free form dance, an evolution of break-dancing that involves striking various physical poses. Generally practiced in gay nightclubs by African and Latin American males, vogue dancers form collectives called "Houses" that perform together. Madonna learned about vogueing from her actor/dancer friend Debi Mazar while she was developing her "Blond Ambition" stage show and looking for street dancers to work with. "Debi told me there was this guy named Luis Ninja who's a spokesperson for the House of Extravaganza," she said. "He got this deejay friend to open another club in the afternoon, brought the whole House of Extravaganza, and they performed for me. They had the lights going, this music pumping. It was just the best dancers you've ever seen, and they were all freestyling."[4]

Like white rapper Vanilla Ice, whom she briefly dated in the early 1990s, Madonna often has been accused of "embodying the white mainstream's commercial appropriation and watering down of traditionally African-American music."[5] Both were influenced by the record industry to exaggerate their ties to the African-American community. Vanilla Ice had manufactured claims that he'd attended an all-black high school; Madonna initially had been marketed as a black singer. Feminist and racial scholar Bell Hooks is especially critical of Madonna's consumer-driven methodology as it applies to borrowing from African-American influences and profiting from them. "It is a very recent historical phenomenon for any white girl to be able to get some mileage out of flaunting her fascination and envy of blackness," she writes in an essay in which she likens Madonna to a plantation mistress. "The thing about envy is that it is always ready to destroy, erase, take-over, and consume the desired object. That's exactly what Madonna attempts to do when she appropriates and commodifies aspects of black culture."[6]

These accusations extend to her appropriation of the gay lifestyle, which some have argued actually undermines alternative gender politics. In the essay "No Sex in *Sex*," professors Donald Crimp and Michael Warner chide Madonna for using the queer aesthetic as a foil to eroticize and glamorize her own image, contending that "Madonna can be as queer as she wants to, but only because we know she's not."[7] Ultimately, however, they admit that Madonna's attempts to represent and normalize what are perceived by the status quo as "subversive" sexual behaviors have not only challenged heterosexuals, but have helped to unite the homosexual community—gays, lesbians, transsexuals, and others alike. "Appropriation is a weird term," Warner writes, "because in a way you always win these battles by being appropriated. If you're going to conquer cultural turf and gain a certain amount of legitimacy, how else is it going to happen except through the appropriation of certain rhetoric by people who haven't hitherto been part of the minority culture?"[8]

Madonna's identification with homosexuals is not, after all, disingenuous. As Professor Crimp points out, "She certainly hangs out with queers enough to have adopted queer style for herself."[9] Her first dance mentor, Christopher Flynn, was gay, as is her brother Christopher, her closest family member and frequent collaborator. Many of her high-profile friends and associates have been bi- or homosexual, including comedienne Sandra Bernhard, artists Keith Haring and Andy Warhol, poet Haoui Montaug, filmmaker Howard Brookner, and nightclub owner Ingrid Casares. Videos for her songs "Justify My Love" and "Erotica" were banned or censored for their explicit content, including portrayal of cross-dressing, sadomasochism, and homosexuality. Further, from the beginning of her career she championed gay rights at a time when it wasn't chic to do so. In the earliest stages of the AIDS epidemic, when little was known about its cause, it was labeled a "homosexual" disease. AIDS victims, and homosexuals in general, were shunned and persecuted. Madonna, however, campaigned actively for AIDS awareness. Having lost many close friends to AIDS, she has donated millions of dollars to projects such the American Foundation for AIDS Research. She consistently participates in fund-raisers such as Live-Aid and Band-Aid among others. A vocal proponent of safe sex, as well, she has been known to add condoms to the per diem pay of employees on tour with her.

Chapter 20

A League of Her Own

How can anything that's captured so many people's imaginations, that's generated so many millions of dollars, how can it fail to interest you? —Professor Douglas Crimp on Madonna[1]

In 1991, Madonna told *The Advocate* magazine that she felt a lot of camaraderie with homosexuals—gay men in particular—and their feelings of persecution and being an outsider. "I'm completely compassionate about their choice in life, their life-style, and I support it," she stated.[2] Her empathy is evident in the tell-all documentary of her "Blond Ambition" tour, *Truth or Dare*, released the same year. The film is similar to D. A. Pennebaker's *Don't Look Back*, which documented Bob Dylan's 1965 concert tour in England. *Don't Look Back* helped to demythologize the life of folk singer/songwriter Bob Dylan to reveal the man behind the music. In turn, *Truth or Dare* "is about more than

Madonna, her brother Christopher Ciccone (left), and director Alek Keshishian (right) pose at a showing of *Truth or Dare*. Madonna has always been close with Christopher, who has often worked with her.

music. It is about what it takes and what it means to be a star. . . . it comes as close as any movie can to capturing her [Madonna's] essence."[3]

Truth or Dare predicated reality television, however the footage spanning the concert tour seems candid and unplanned with a few exceptions. Madonna purportedly allowed director Alek Keshishian complete access onstage and off, to chronicle the experience of life on the road with her and her entourage. She encouraged him and his camera crew to be intrusive and unsparing as they probed the behind-the-scenes drama that unfolded as the tour progressed. The result does not always flatter its subject matter. We see a spectrum of Madonnas—generous to insensitive, companionable to vulgar. "It is extremely realistic. It is Madonna as I know her," commented her brother Christopher.[4]

The invasion bordered on exploitation. Some reviewers believed those nearest Madonna paid the price for her desire for self-promotion and publicity. They expressed concern for the plight of the tour dancers "whose vulnerability she admits to exploiting in order to play the mother-figure."[5] Others held another view. They found the documentary innovative, praising it for its groundbreaking perspective of gay culture. "It's hard to think of another film about a non-gay subject in which the presence of gay people is not only normal and accepted but treasured. Of her seven dancers, all are ethnic minorities, and all but one are gay. Madonna clearly identifies with them, camping and partying and flirting with them freely."[6]

"What I loved about *Truth or Dare*," agreed Michael Warner, "was the way it was playing into the cultural battles over censorship at the time. It seemed to me an important response to the then-ascendant rhetoric of PC [political correctness] and family values."[7]

Three of the dancers did, in fact, sue Madonna over the movie. When asked if she'd gone too far or revealed too much, Madonna attributed this attitude to general overreaction to her work. "Life is about the highs and the lows, and if you just present the mids, then what's the point?" she explained. "These issues [in the film] are dealt with in drama all of the time," she continued, "but I think the hard thing for people to take will be that there isn't someone playing the part of my life in a movie fifty years from now when I'm dead. I'm doing it myself. No one has ever done that before."[8]

Madonna's next move was to form her own $60 million multimedia enterprise, Maverick Entertainment. It would enable Madonna, as CEO, to develop her own books, film, video, records, TV, and related merchandise. Maverick's first venture was *Sex*, a partly autobiographical coffee table book written by Madonna. In diary format, she takes on the character of Mistress Dita,[9] based on Dita Parlo, a silent movie actress, the dominatrix "love technician," whose ruminations on sex guide the reader through the book. Dita pens in the introduction to the book: "This book is about sex.

Sex is not love. Love is not sex. But the best of both
worlds is created when they come together. . .
Everything you are about to see and read is a fantasy,
a dream, pretend. . . "[10] One hundred and twenty-eight
photos accompany the text, shot by Steven Meisel,
who had collaborated with Madonna on fashion
magazine spreads. He photographed her alone and
in compromising positions with pizza slices, gasoline
pumps, dogs, skinheads, and male strippers. Celebrities
such as Vanilla Ice, Naomi Campbell, Isabella Rossellini,
and Big Daddy Kane also posed with her.

The text and photos focus on sexual pleasure,
depicting bondage, nudity, fondling, kissing, but no
penetration. Spiral bound between sheets of metal,
sheathed in mylar with added goodies such as an
"Erotica" song sampler and a comic book, *Sex* cost $50.
Marketed as an art book, albeit an erotic one, it was
sold in regular bookstores. This outraged a mix of
feminists, liberals, and conservatives worldwide. *Sex*
was condemned as pornography and banned in several
states and countries. The backlash against Madonna
included hate mail and death threats. In her essay
"Talking About *Sex*," Carol A. Queen dismisses this
barrage of condemnation, "To the sexually adventurous
female, the message sent by critics of *Sex* seems sticky
with prurience and judgement. Madonna is called
an exhibitionist as if that were a problem and not an
inspiration; a pathology rather than a source of pleasure
. . . Perhaps the problem here is that Madonna's

exhibitionism is being viewed as an economic strategy and a personality disorder not just a sexual flavor."[11]

Maverick, which had lived up to the promise of non-conformity inherent in its name, weathered the criticism surprisingly well. Despite (or perhaps because of) the controversy, *Sex* was a commercial success. It sold 150,000 copies on its first day of release in the United States and 500,000 the first week. One and a half million copies sold around the globe, generating a net profit of almost $20 million. The maverick behind Maverick, however, considered it a turning point in her career.

Chapter 21

You Must Love Me

After the scandal of her book, *Sex*, Madonna's career mellowed a bit, though it did not slow down. Madonna describes the years between 1992 and 1996 as those in which her "skin grew at least six inches thick."[1] "I do think that society tends to root for you to win or lose," she said. "It's kind of tragic, in a way, because what goes up must come down. Anyone who attains an enormous popularity is about to see what the bottom of a boot looks like."[2]

She continued to produce chart-topping albums such as *Erotica* and *Bedtime Stories*, and acted in a number of somewhat undistinguished movies such as *A League of Their Own* and Woody Allen's *Shadows and Fog*. Her biggest successes during this period, however, were as CEO of Maverick. Maverick Records fared well, signing top-notch performer Alanis Morissette among others. *Dangerous Game*, the first movie financed by her production company, attracted seasoned veterans

Harvey Keitel, James Russo, and director Abel Ferrara. Though panned by many critics, the *New York Times* gave the experimental film a positive review, calling it a "scorching psychodrama." They noted Madonna's demure performance.[3]

In 1993, Madonna launched the "Girlie Show," a cabaret tour staged like a circus and designed and choreographed by her brother Christopher. In "Girlie Show," Madonna reprised her Dita character, serving as Mistress of Ceremonies throughout the two-hour burlesque. She set the tone in the opening act, brandishing a ringmaster's whip while topless acrobats performed a pole dance. Those who missed the humor in her *Sex* book could not fail to catch the parody and exaggeration in this decadent show. "Madonna's whole career up to and including *Sex* has depended heavily on camp imagery and camp understandings of gender and sex,"[4] writes sex educator Carol A. Queen, whose own career is centered on the idea that "we have to remove the stigma from sex before we can make it fabulous."[5] The term *camp* in this context means a style of creative expression that is absurdly exaggerated and often combines elements of pop culture.

While the exaggerations of camp may have characterized "Girlie Show," a sellout around the world, Madonna sought a meatier comeback. She single-handedly pursued the starring role in the film version of Andrew Lloyd Webber and Tim Rice's 1978 rock opera *Evita*, based loosely on the life of Evá Perón, the wife of

Argentinian dictator Juan Perón. Madonna saw many parallels between herself and Evá Perón (nicknamed Evita). Whereas Madonna is a cultural icon in the United States, Evita is revered as Argentina's national saint. Born in poverty, through drive and ambition she transformed herself into a glamorous radio star who, like Madonna, hungered for mass adulation. It was in the political arena, however, that she gained her fame after marrying Perón. Her popularity and identification with the working class helped secure him the presidency in 1946. Their regime was, unfortunately, suspect. Perón and Evita lived an extravagant lifestyle, hoarding nearly as much money as they lavished on the poor through lotteries and work projects. Evita died of ovarian cancer in 1952 at the age of thirty-three.

Director Alan Parker was reluctant to cast Madonna in the movie, given her less than stellar reputation at the box office. Oscar winning lyricist Tim Rice championed her, however, aware that her look, personality, and singing and dancing talent made for a more plausible Evita than the bevy of screen actresses up for the role. "I think she's a fine artist and I was very keen for her to get the part, rather than some of the other ladies who would have been interesting but I don't think would have been right like Meryl Streep and Michelle Pfeiffer and other names that were tossed around," he said.[6]

Madonna poured herself into the role, studying Evita's life and affecting her physical appearance and mannerisms. Since the movie is an opera, with complex musical arrangements and virtually no speaking lines, she strengthened her voice through singing lessons and learned how to dance the tango. She also fought with Rice and Parker to humanize her character, which she believed was conceived somewhat unsympathetically. "I think that a person who attained the kind of power she attained and accomplished what she accomplished could not be stupid or just opportunistic," she explained. "You've got to have something going on up there."[7] Madonna did not always get her way. She lobbied unsuccessfully to change the lyrics of Rice's new song, "You Must Love Me," which went on to win an Academy Award. Still her efforts paid off handsomely. She carried the movie, receiving a Golden Globe Award for her strong performance.

Though extremely rewarding, making the movie proved arduous for Madonna. *Evita* was filmed in three countries—Argentina, Britain, and Hungary—and paparazzi followed her everywhere, sometimes hiding underneath her car to photograph her as she climbed inside. In Argentina the project was unpopular. Protesters who were offended that she was cast in the role of their national hero routinely harassed her. "When we were in Argentina," confirmed *Evita* co-star Antonio Banderas, "half of the people were hating her and half of the people were loving her. It was really the story all over again of Eva Duarte [Perón's maiden name]."[8]

Near the end of the filming, Madonna discovered that she was pregnant. "I felt that it was kind of poetic that it happened while I was trying to give birth to another sort of baby," she told a reporter.[9] Since her divorce, Madonna's love life had been a circus. She juggled celebrity boyfriends such as Warren Beatty, Vanilla Ice, and Dennis Rodman with employee conquests such as Tony Ward (who appeared in several of her videos) and her bodyguard Jim Albright. Her name was also romantically linked with Sandra Bernhard, Ingrid Casares, and model Jenny Shimizu.

Her current love was neither a celebrity nor an employee, but rather a Manhattan personal trainer and actor named Carlos Leon. Handsome, muscular, with dark curly hair and a Latin complexion, Madonna pursued him after an encounter while both were jogging in Central Park. Before her pregnancy, theirs had been a low-key love affair. The pregnancy was unplanned but both were excited by the prospect of parenthood. At thirty-eight, Madonna was eager to have a child. On October 14, 1996, she gave birth to a beautiful, dark-headed baby, Lourdes Maria Ciccone Leon.

Chapter 22

Open Your Heart to Me

Despite accusations that Carlos Leon was merely a "sperm donor," he and Madonna had dated for two years before her pregnancy and seemed very content with each other. But though Carlos Leon maintains a significant presence in Lourdes's life, he did not remain Madonna's beau for very long after Lourdes was born. Madonna settled with Lourdes in California, and Leon's ties were in New York. They ended their relationship in 1997; parting company as good friends and co-parents. Madonna then entered a very spiritual phase. "The whole idea of giving birth and being responsible for another life put me in a different place, a place I'd never been before," she said at the time. "I feel like I'm starting my life over in some ways. My daughter's birth was like a rebirth for me."[1]

Madonna told talk-show host Larry King that being a mother to Lourdes was more than what she thought it would be. "Every day I am in complete wonderment of her . . . I love looking into her eyes. I love watching her grow. I love watching her absorb life around her."[2] Leon's heritage is Cuban, and Lourdes is a popular Cuban name. It is also a name that Madonna linked to her mother, who received holy water from Lourdes, France, when she was dying of cancer. Madonna considered Lourdes (or Lola as she is nicknamed) to be a healing influence in her life similar to water, which she likened to a healing element. "There's water in birth and there's water in baptism and when you go into the bath or in the ocean there's a feeling of cleansing, a feeling of starting all over again. Being new, being healed. That's sort of what's going on in my life and I'm exploring that element in my songwriting," she said in 1998.[3]

Motherhood seemed to deepen Madonna's serenity and her artistic convictions. According to Ingrid Sischy of *Vanity Fair* magazine, "Having a baby gave her, at the very least, what she calls 'a moment of stillness' when she was forced to allow herself to slow down, step away, and surrender."[4] *Ray of Light*, a record released in 1998, embodied this new inner calm. During production, Madonna left herself open to experimentation. Desiring to update her dance tunes with a European sensibility, an ethereal sonic texture that she couldn't achieve with live musicians, she chose to collaborate with British musician and producer William Orbit, an underground electronic artist. Unlike the past, she entered the studio without a set idea of what the music would sound like. Madonna stated,

Madonna's experiments with electronic sound paid off when she collected four Grammy Awards for her album *Ray of Light* in 1999.

> I let William [Orbit] play Mad Professor. He comes
> from a very experimental, cutting-edge sort of
> place—he's not a trained musician, and I'm used
> to working with classically trained musicians—but
> I knew that's where I wanted to go, so I took a lot
> more risks. Oftentimes the creative process was
> frustrating because I wasn't used to it; it took
> longer than usual to make this record. But I realize
> now that I needed that time to get where I was
> going.[5]

Orbit's electronic sound perfectly married the themes
of rebirth, redemption, mysticism, and spirituality that
Madonna wanted to explore through the album. She had
been listening to world music including North African
and Indian music, so Orbit programmed Eastern
instruments such as the sitar, rebana, and tabla into the
recordings. Madonna's spiritual journey also influenced
the album. Although Madonna was raised Catholic, she
rejected many of its principles. Her interest in spiritual
philosophy, though, had never waned. Through the
years, she had studied Eastern religions such as
Hinduism and Buddhism. While pregnant with Lourdes,
she began practicing yoga and Kabbalah, an ancient
Jewish doctrine that likewise promotes unity and inner
harmony, both of which helped her to make peace with
herself. Her yogic practices led her to study Sanskrit, a
language she uses in the song "Shanti/Ashtangi."

The result was a critical and commercial triumph,
securing Madonna artistic accolades and four Grammy
Awards. She followed her success with *Music*, working
again with Orbit as well as French producer Mirwais

Ahmadzai. Her new synth-heavy, technology-driven musical direction earned Madonna the title "Veronica Electronica." Veronica is Madonna's confirmation name, the name she chose for herself as a preteen when she underwent the Roman Catholic sacrament of verifying her membership in the church. While discussing her religious affiliation, Madonna explained, "In terms of saints, when I was confirmed I took the name Veronica because she wiped the face of Jesus. You know, you weren't supposed to help Christ while he was on his way to the Crucifixion; she was not afraid to step out and wipe the sweat off him and help him. So I liked her for doing that, and I took her name."[6]

In 1998, Madonna was still an unwed mother. Lyrics from *Ray of Light*'s, "Has To Be," speak of her yearnings for a partner or soul mate. They assert her belief that she would connect with someone who existed in the world just for her. She was right, of course, and "Veronica Electronica" would soon meet the man whose name she was destined to step out with.

That same year, Trudi Styler, wife of legendary rock vocalist Sting, co-produced the independent film about British gangsters, *Lock, Stock and Two Smoking Barrels*. In the summer, she invited Madonna, a long-time friend of the family, to visit her at her English residence to discuss a possible soundtrack album. She arranged for the film's director, Guy Ritchie, to sit next to Madonna at lunch. Though Madonna's involvement in the soundtrack album didn't pan out, a romance between her and Ritchie did.

An artist, writer, and innovative film director, Guy Ritchie, ruggedly handsome and ten years her junior, immediately captured Madonna's interest. He shares her first husband's intensity and focus, along with a similar bad-boy image. For Madonna, it was love at first sight. He apparently stopped her in her tracks. After their first meeting, she later said, "I went into a state of denial because he lived here and I lived in America and wasn't interested in torturing myself by having some long-distance love affair. But it happened anyway. It was just one of those . . . inexplicable uncontrollable things."[7]

Despite a rocky start—an on again/off again battle of wills—she committed herself to him. His independent nature, coupled with his willingness to resist her domination, made him irresistible to her. Several tracks on her *Music* album, particularly "Amazing" and "I Deserve It," were essentially love songs to Ritchie. They refer to the destiny of two people's lives converging upon each other.

Ritchie refused to leave Europe, where his career was centered. Therefore, in 2000, Madonna uprooted her entourage and moved to London. She was willing to sacrifice to make things work for all involved, scheduling transatlantic visits so that she could maintain her business interests in the states, and Lourdes could still spend time with her father. "There are many days when I feel like a stranger in a strange land and I despair," Madonna nevertheless said of her move. "I miss my friends and I miss certain things that one always misses about the country of their origin. But I love the idea—whether it's in my work or where I live— exploring new frontier."[8]

On August 11, 2000, Madonna gave birth to Rocco, her son by Ritchie. Rocco was born prematurely, and had to stay in an incubator for five days. Madonna returned home with the baby on her forty-second birthday to find a paper bag lying atop her nightstand. Inside, Ritchie had put a gift box with a diamond ring and a marriage proposal. "He wrote to me about everything we've been through, my birthday and the baby and how happy he was," recalled Madonna.[9]

Four months later Rocco was baptized in a thirteenth-century cathedral in Dornoch, Scotland. The next day, on December 22, 2000, Madonna and Ritchie exchanged wedding vows in Scotland's Skibo Castle. Thanks to private security, the ceremony was a grand and uninterrupted one. It followed a traditional Church of Scotland wedding sequence, including a reading of vows written by the couple. Ritchie wore a green-tartan hunting kilt, in honor of his family's Macintosh clan. Two best men represented him—film producer Matthew Vaughan and London nightclub owner Piers Adam. Chlóe designer Stella McCartney, daughter of Paul McCartney, who designed Madonna's ivory silk, strapless wedding gown, was maid of honor. Lourdes served as the flower girl. The Reverend Susan Brown,

Madonna waved to the crowd as Guy Ritchie held their son, Rocco, after his baptism in 2000. Ritchie and Madonna would marry the next day.

a groundbreaking female minister, presided.[10] She later confirmed the matrimony to the press. Her gift to the couple was a twin pack of toilet paper. It symbolized her desire for Madonna and Guy to experience "a soft, long, and durable marriage."[11]

Guests described Madonna as looking "like a princess" in an antique lace veil held in place by an Edwardian diamond tiara.[12] After the wedding, she threw her bouquet at the ladies and tossed her garter to the men. The guest list read like a celebrity who's who, among them Sting, Trudi Styler, Gwyneth Paltrow, Debi Mazar, Rupert Everett, Donatella Versace, Carlos Leon, and members of the bride and groom's family. They feasted on lobster, salmon, mussels, Aberdeen angus beef, roast potatoes, and red cabbage, then toasted the bride and groom. Piers Adam's toast included a slideshow of photos from Ritchie's childhood. Later in the evening, the bridal party and guests danced in the castle basement, set up as a disco. The DJ, Miami's Tracy Young, who would later remix Madonna albums *Music* and *Confessions on a Dance Floor*, spun hits by Sting and Madonna.[13]

Chapter 23

Time Goes So Slowly

As soon as you figure something out, there's
something a lot harder you've got to go to next.
It's actually a good metaphor for life.
　　　—Madonna, referring to Ashtanga yoga[1]

After her picture perfect wedding, Madonna set out
once again to conquer the world. Her "Drowned World"
tour played forty-eight cities in arena stages around
the globe and showcased songs on her *Ray of Light*
and *Music* albums. Madonna's presence in this tour
is noticeably defiant. She replaces the camp (and a
lot of the warmth and humor) of her other shows with
rock star attitude and avant-garde self-consciousness.
Through her stark lyrics, belligerent electric guitar solos,
in-your-face banter, and violent choreography, she sets
out "to intimidate the audience as much as to entertain
them," wrote one reporter. "With a list of dark 'n' arty
references ranging from manga [anime] videos to Derek

Jarman's ancient punk film *Jubilee*, this was never going to be a feel-good Greatest Hits show."[2]

The special effects and imagery are at once striking and sobering—a complete contrast to the *Music* promotional tour, "Rock N Roll Circus," which was much lighter in tone. "I feel that the 'Drowned World' tour was a statement of who she had evolved into," tour director and choreographer Jamie King articulated. "You had to have that dark version, a very introspective and heavy version of her, to be able to get to this next place which was the "Re-Invention" tour."[3]

Madonna's "Re-Invention" tour took place three years later in 2004 and netted her $125 million. It seemed to mark a return to a more fan-friendly performance with much less distance between Madonna and her audience literally and figuratively. Enormous screens projected Madonna and her dancers live, but also played prerecorded dance routines that complemented the onstage action. Suspended catwalks allowed Madonna to venture out into the crowd. King disagrees with the assumption that the tour was conceived along these lines to address "Drowned World's" relative inaccessibility. King explained, "I think that Madonna first and foremost is always going to do what she feels is right for the time, for her. I don't think Madonna, although she loves and adores her fans, ever does anything for them specifically at a request, if you know what I mean. She's more about inspiring them and inspiring the world. So with that you can't always do what you're told. You have to be a leader not a follower. . . . She's an artist. Madonna is a true artist. She has to be able to explore and become what she is at that moment. She was the "Re-Invention" tour at the time of the "Re-Invention" tour. She was the "Drowned World" tour at the time of that tour."[4]

Songwriter Joe Henry, Madonna's brother-in-law, once aptly likened the quick pace of Madonna's concerts to a parade. For "Re-Invention," King designed the staging and choreography to specifically reflect perpetual motion. He wanted to give the impression of continual progression—one surprise after the other. "One minute she's provocatively vogueing with her male dancers while homo-erotic images flash behind her, the next she's in fatigues, twirling a rifle to the sounds of explosions and helicopters. In the blink of an eye she goes from being strapped in an electric chair to pulling up her kilt to spell the word "FREEDOM" with glitter letters on her and her dancers' underpants," said one reporter covering the tour's kick-off.[5] According to fan Matthew Hunt, "The show was a sensory overload, with constant video projections, a moving stage, fire-jugglers, break-dancers, and skateboarders."[6]

It was also retrospective, reexamining hits spanning Madonna's career from a post-9/11 perspective, including her single "American Life." In this rap ditty, she questions the shallowness of modern life and the American Dream under President George W. Bush's conservative watch. Before the tour, this song had

129

generated a lot of controversy given the tense political climate of the United States, embroiled in an unpopular conflict with Iraq. Intended "to convey strong anti-war, anti-materialism and anti-fashion industry statements,"[7] the *American Life* video proliferated with militaristic images—flags, fighter jets, mushroom clouds. Soldiers and refugees model fashion fatigues as they strut down a runway. At the end, Madonna tosses a fake grenade to a George Bush look-alike who uses it to light his cigar.

Worried that its message would be perceived as anti-American, Madonna withdrew the original video from MTV circulation before its national premiere in 2003. She stated her rationale as follows: "I have decided not to release my new video. It was filmed before the war [with Iraq] started and I do not believe it is appropriate to air it at this time. Due to the volatile state of the world and out of sensitivity and respect to the armed forces, who I support and pray for, I do not want to risk offending anyone who might misinterpret the meaning of this video."[8]

The "Re-Invention" tour was so-named to poke fun at Madonna's many incarnations—incarnations she previously had no qualms about offending others with. Soon she would attempt yet another change. In 2004, Madonna announced her intention to adopt a new name, Esther, after the biblical queen celebrated during the Jewish festival Purim. Though the name did not stay with her very long, the gesture reflected her deepening attachment to Kabbalah, a belief system she had studied for many years. "One of the central aspects to the study of Kabbalah," she has said, "is the idea that we are responsible for our behavior, we are responsible for everything that happens to us. It's very liberating not to think of yourself as a victim. So I like that aspect. That has freed me enormously."[9]

By changing her name, Madonna had wanted to attach new energy to her person. She was now a happily married wife with two children. Besides being a diva, she ran a tidy business and home life. "Even my children have to clean up their mess, clean up their rooms," she is quoted as saying. "Manners, 'thank you,' 'please,' 'take your dishes to the sink.' I mean . . . gratitude, being grateful—that is—that has to happen. . . If it's traditional to be a decent human being, then I'm traditional."[10]

> "Even my children have to clean up their mess."

These traditional values included fostering her children's imaginations by encouraging them to read books instead of watching television. As a child, Madonna had not been allowed to watch television. Books such as *Alice in Wonderland*, *Charlotte's Web*, and the *Chronicles of Narnia* had been her fondest escape. Yet wading through contemporary children's literature with Lola and Rocco proved discouraging for her. She wasn't satisfied with the content of most of the books they were reading. Instead of complaining, her teacher at the Kabbalah center suggested that she act.

131

Throughout her career, Madonna has been a prolific writer as her many songwriting credits can attest. She keeps a pillow book of ideas (a diary or journal), jotting down dreams or poems or things she reads in books and clipping out articles that she wants to remember from newspapers. Pillow book in hand, with memories of the bedtime stories her father would improvise for her and her eight siblings, she decided to branch into children's fiction. Madonna contracted with Penguin Books to write her own series of five picture books. "I sit in front of the computer and stick my little statue, who's my writing muse, next to my computer and, OK, I'm going to write—and it comes," she explained of her writing process.[11] In September 2003, her first children's book, *English Roses* was published in thirty languages and distributed in one hundred countries. It immediately topped the *New York Times* bestseller list for children. *Mr. Peabody's Apples*, *Yakov and the Seven Thieves*, and *The Adventures of Abdi* soon followed. *Lotsa de Casha*, her fifth, saw print in June 2005.

Veteran children's authors, such as Jane Yolen, dismissed Madonna's efforts, unhappy that she had joined the bandwagon of celebrity authors. "What really gripes me," Yolen complained, "is when someone like Madonna gets on national television and says [something like], 'I had to write my book because there weren't any good children's books out there.'"[12]

All of Madonna's books, however, are beautifully designed and illustrated. Her stories carry clear morals

Madonna reads *Lotsa De Casha* to a group of children at a New York bookstore in 2005. Though some prominent children's authors have criticized Madonna's work, her books have been wildly popular.

about the power of words or the importance of helping others. "I feel like everything we do—the movies we make, the music, the stuff that's on television—affects society in a potent way," she said. "I feel a sense of responsibility because my consciousness has been raised and I would like to impart the wisdom I have to others without being corny or preachy."[13]

Marriage and motherhood clearly have altered Madonna's priorities. This is most evident when watching *Let Me Tell You a Secret*, the documentary of her "Re-Invention" tour. The film captures a mature and centered woman. It is the companion to *Truth or Dare*, which was made during her "Blond Ambition" tour. No longer "working out publicly [her] confusion about [her] own sexuality," Madonna has learned to differentiate between family and work, personal life and celebrity.[14] "It's a different me," she said. "I have a husband, I have a family, my whole life has changed. It would be pretty strange if I was behaving the same way I did 12 years ago—that would be a little freaky."[15]

That said, in 2005 Madonna returned to the music of her childhood with her fourteenth album, *Confessions on a Dance Floor*, an homage to 1970s disco. Pounding beats and sassy lyrics married nostalgic tracks from disco groups Abba and the BeeGees with remix technology that allowed Madonna to be her own backup singer. Her "Confessions" tour the following summer resembled a theme party with lots of disco balls and dancing. "I'm going to turn the world into one big dance floor," she said.[16]

> "... if I was behaving the same way I did 12 years ago— that would be a little freaky."

The tour proved to be yet another profitable venture for Madonna, demonstrating her continued worldwide popularity. However, it also showed that Madonna would not shy away from controversy as she approached the age of fifty.

Madonna received criticism from members of the Roman Catholic church in the United States, Europe, and Asia for a segment of her performance during which she staged a mock crucifixion. Madonna descended to the stage on a glittered, mirrored, suspended cross while wearing a fake crown of thorns. Despite protests, Madonna would not change her show, even while performing roughly a mile from the Vatican when the tour reached Rome.

"It is disrespectful, in bad taste and provocative," said Father Manfredo Leone from Rome's Santa Maria Liberatrice church. "Being raised on a cross with a crown of thorns like a modern Christ is absurd. Doing it in the cradle of Christianity comes close to blasphemy."[17]

Vatican Cardinal Ersilio Tonino, supported by the Pope, went so far as to call for Madonna to be excommunicated.[18]

While the stunt did not keep fans from flocking to her shows, some of them questioned its inclusion. However, after so many years of stirring the pot, fans were no longer surprised by Madonna causing controversy.

"The crucifixion was unnecessary and provocative. Because this is Rome, I wish she'd cut it out. But it's Madonna, she's an icon, and that balances out her need to provoke," said Roman Tonia Valerio.[19]

In addition to offending large segments of the population during the summer of 2006, Madonna was also busy figuring out how to help those in need. She decided to assist orphans in Malawi, Africa, a nation in the southeastern part of the continent that is plagued by AIDS and malaria, and has about 1 million orphans.[20]

Madonna aimed to raise at least $3 million for the Raising Malawi project, which she and Kabbalah Center founder Michael Berg co-founded. She met with former President Bill Clinton, and planned to finance a $1 million documentary about the difficulties facing the orphans. Finally, Madonna formed a partnership with Dr. Jeffrey Sachs, an anti-poverty champion, to improve the health, agriculture, and economy of a Malawi village.[21]

> **"We don't realize there's a bigger system at work. Everything that comes to you is for a reason."**

"Now that I have children and now that I have what I consider to be a better perspective on life, I have felt responsible for the children of the world," Madonna said. "I've been doing bits and bobs about it and I suppose I was looking for a big, big project I could sink my teeth into."[22]

Though Madonna had yet to visit the country, August 2006 witnessed the groundbreaking of an orphan-care center in Malawi that would be able to feed and educate up to 1,000 children a day.[23]

Madonna is most famous for being Madonna. From albums and tours, to movies, books, and merchandise such as ring tones, she represents big business. She insists, however, that she is still a rebel concerned about serious issues and about making an impact on the world with her art. Madonna believes, she says, that her real responsibility is "to bring light to the world and make the world a better place . . . Because what is a rebel?

It's someone who thinks outside the box—someone who doesn't subscribe to any program. . . We don't realize there's a bigger system at work. Everything that comes to you is for a reason. And I think that's really revolutionary, because we are not trained to think that in our society."[24]

Selected Discography of Madonna

Albums

1983 *Madonna*

1984 *Like A Virgin*

1985 *Vision Quest*

1986 *True Blue*

1987 *Who's That Girl?* (Soundtrack)

   You Can Dance (Remix Album)

1989 *Like A Prayer*

1990 *The Immaculate Collection* (Compilation)

   I'm Breathless (Soundtrack)

1992 *Erotica*

1994 *Bedtime Stories*

1995 *Something to Remember* (Compilation)

1996 *Evita* (Soundtrack)

1998 *Ray of Light*

2000 *Music*

2001 *GHV2* (Compilation)

2003 *American Life*

2003 *Remixed & Revisited* (Remix Album)

2005 *Confessions on a Dance Floor*

2006 *I'm Going to Tell You a Secret* (Live Album)

Concert Tours

1985 The Virgin Tour

1987 Who's That Girl Tour

1990 Blond Ambition Tour

1993 The Girlie Show

2001 Drowned World Tour

2004 The Re-Invention Tour

2006 Confessions Tour

Chapter Notes

Chapter 1. I Feel It in Your Kiss

1. Robert Holfer, "An Affair to Remember: Madonna Makes Love to the Camera," *Life*, December 1986, p. 50.

2. "The Day That Beta Died: Farewell to Sony Betamax," August 28, 2002, <http://www.betainfoguide.com/Betadied.htm> (January 6, 2006).

3. Denise Worrell, "Now: Madonna on Madonna," *TIME*, May 27, 1985, <http://www.time.com/time/archive/printout/0,23657,957025,00.html> (August 3, 2006).

4. Joel D. Schwarz, "Virgin Territory: How Madonna Straddles Innocence and Decadence," *The New Republic, Inc.*, August 26, 1985, pp. 30–33.

5. Gavin Mueller, "Pop Playground: MTV VMA Wrap-up," *stylusmagazine.com*, September 2, 2003, <http://www.stylusmagazine.com/article/pop_playground/the-2003-vma-wrap-up.htm> (August 4, 2006).

6. Tucker Carlson, "Britney Would Not Kiss Another Woman Besides Madonna," September 4, 2003, <http://www.cnn.com/2003/SHOWBIZ/Music/09/03/britney.spears/> (January 6, 2006).

7. "Madonna says daughter asked if she was gay," *Associated Press*, March 6, 2006, <http://www.mercurynews.com/mld/mercurynews/entertainment/gossip/14032911.htm> (July 19, 2006).

8. Sarah Warn, "VMA's Madonna-Britney-Christina Kiss: Progress or Publicity Stunt?," September 2004, <http://www.afterellen.com/TV/vmakiss.html> (July 19, 2006).

Chapter 2. What It Feels Like for a Girl

1. Ingrid Sischy, "From the editor's desk: February 2004: a conversation between Ingrid Sischy and Camille Paglia," *Interview Magazine*, February 2, 2004, <http://www.findarticles.com/p/articles/mi_m1285/is_1_34/ai_112482974/pg_2> (January 6, 2006).

2. Jennifer Egan, "You Don't Know Madonna," December 2002, <http://www.jenniferegan.com/articles/2002_12_gq_madonna.html> (January 6, 2006).

3. Ibid.

4. James Combs, *Phony Culture: Confidence and Malaise in Contemporary America* (Bowling Green, OH: Bowling Green State University Popular Press, 1994), p. 75.

5. Ibid.

6. Jay Jimenez, "Interview," *Next Magazine*, February 2000, <http://www.madonna-online.ch/m-online/interviews/interview-sites/00-02_next-magazine-interview.htm> (January 6, 2006).

7. Gabriella, "Bubble Gum Princess Gone Serene Queen," *NY Rock*, August 1998, <http://www.nyrock.com/interviews/madonna_int.htm> (July 19, 2006).

8. Jay Jimenez, "Interview, " *Next Magazine*.

9. Michael J. Hurd, "Britney Spears-Madonna Kiss," *Capitalism Magazine*, September 10, 2003, <http://www.capmag.com/article.asp?ID=3103> (July 19, 2006).

10. Danny Eccleston, "Interview (March '98)," *Q Magazine*, March 1998, <http://www.madonna-online.ch/m-online/interviews/interview-sites/98-03_q-interview.htm> (September 28, 2005).

11. Ingrid Sischy, "Soon to Tour For the First Time in Eight Years, She's Ready to Take on the World," *Interview Magazine*, March 2001, <http://www.findarticles.com/p/articles/mi_m1285/is_3_31/ai_71562921> (September 28, 2005).

12. "J. Randy Taraborrelli—Madonna Biographer," *CNN.com*, July 19, 2001, <http://archives.cnn.com/2001/SHOWBIZ/Music/07/19/randy.taraborrelli.cnna/> (September 28, 2005).

13. Britney Spears, "Madonna," *Rolling Stone Magazine*, n.d., <http://www.rollingstone.com/news/story/_/id/5940017?rnd=1136314579859&has-player=true&version=6.0.11.847> (September 28, 2005).

Chapter 3. Mother and Father

1. Cole J. Cocks, "Madonna Draws a Line: After MTV Rejects her latest Video, the Material Girl Launches a Program of Self Defense and Self-Promotion," *TIME*, December 17, 1990.

2. "News Archive: January 2005," *madonnalicious.com*, n.d., <http://www.madonnalicious.com/archive/january2005.html> (September 28, 2005).

3. Andrew Morton, *Madonna* (New York: St. Martin's Press, 2001), p. 29.

4. Denise Worrell, "Now: Madonna on Madonna," *TIME*, May 27, 1985, <http://www.time.com/time/archive/printout/0,23657,957025,00.html> (August 3, 2006).

5. Morton, p. 30.

6. Denise Worrell, "Now: Madonna on Madonna."

7. Morton, p. 104.

8. Ibid.

9. Ibid., p. 21.

10. Jane Stevenson, "Madonna's Metamorphosis Complete," *Toronto Sun*, March 1, 1998, <http://www.canoe.ca/AllPop-Madonna/cd_rayoflight2.html> (September 28, 2005).

Chapter 4. Papa Don't Preach

1. "Madonna Ciccone Quotes," *www.brainyquote.com*, n.d., <http://www.brainyquote.com/quotes/authors/m/madonna_ciccone.html> (September 28, 2005).

2. Andrew Morton, *Madonna* (New York: St. Martin's Press, 2001), p. 43.

3. "Madonna and Child: The New Baby, the New Life," *Vanity Fair*, March 1998, <http://www.fortunecity.com/tinpan/underworld/437/vf.htm#> (September 28, 2005).

4. Nicole Claro, *Madonna* (New York: Chelsea House Publishers, 1998), p. 24.

5. Denise Worrell, "Now: Madonna on Madonna," *TIME*, May 27, 1985, <http://www.time.com/time/archive/printout/0,23657,957025,00.html> (August 3, 2006).

6. Claro.

7. "Madonna and Child: The New Baby, the New Life," *Vanity Fair*.

8. Steven Holden, "Madonna Goes Heavy on Heart," *New York Times*, June 29, 1986.

9. Becky Johnston, "Confessions of a Catholic Girl," *Interview Magazine*, 1989.

10. Barbara Victor, *Goddess: Inside Madonna* (Harper Collins: New York, 2001), p. 154.

11. Don Shewey, "Madonna: The Saint, the Slut, the Sensation," *The Advocate*, 1991, <http://www.donshewey.com/music_articles/madonna1.htm> (August 4, 2006).

12. Claro, p. 26.

13. John Skow, "Madonna Rocks the Land: Sassy, brassy and beguiling, she laughs her way to fame," *TIME*, May 1985, <http://www.allaboutmadonna.com/press_1985_time.php> (January 6, 2006).

Chapter 5. Causing a Commotion

1. "Madonna Biography," *Madonna Mega website*, n.d., <http://madonnamega.tripod.com/> (September 28, 2005).

2. *Rolling Stone Magazine*, July 1998, <http://www.fortunecity.com/tinpan/underworld/437/rs.htm> (September 28, 2005).

3. Larry King, "Madonna Reviews Life," *Larry King Live*, n.d., <http://www.cnn.com/SHOWBIZ/Music/9901/19/madonna.lkl/> (July 19, 2006).

4. "Madonna and Child, The New Baby, The New Life," *Vanity Fair*, March 1998, <http://www.fortunecity.com/tinpan/underworld/437/vf.htm> (September 28, 2005).

5. Denise Worrell, "Now: Madonna on Madonna," *TIME*, May 27, 1985, <http://www.time.com/time/archive/printout/0,23657,957025,00.html> (August 3, 2006).

6. Andrew Morton, *Madonna* (New York: St. Martin's Press, 2001), pp. 52–53.

Chapter 6. You Can Dance, for Inspiration

1. "Madonna: She's One Lucky Star!," *Teen Magazine*, 1984.

2. Denise Worrell, "Now: Madonna on Madonna," *TIME*, May 27, 1985, <http://www.time.com/time/archive/printout/0,23657,957025,00.html> (August 3, 2006).

3. Nicole Claro, *Madonna* (New York: Chelsea House Publishers, 1998), p. 29.

4. "Vladimir Dokoudovsky (1919–1998)," n.d., <http://michaelminn.net/andros/biographies/dokoudovsky_vladimir.htm> (September 28, 2005).

5. Andrew Morton, *Madonna* (New York: St. Martin's Press, 2001), p. 57.

6. Stephen Holden, "Madonna Goes Heavy on Heart," *New York Times*, June 29, 1986.

7. Morton, p. 57.

8. Morton, p. 164.

9. Don Shewey, "Madonna: The Saint, the Slut, the Sensation," *The Advocate*, 1991, <http://www.donshewey.com/music_articles/madonna1.htm> (July 19, 2006).

10. Ibid.

11. Ibid.

12. Barbara Victor, *Goddess: Inside Madonna* (New York: Harper Collins, Inc, 2001).

Chapter 7. **You'll See**

1. Denise Worrell, "Now: Madonna on Madonna," *TIME*, May 27, 1985, <http://www.time.com/time/archive/printout/0,23657,957025,00.html> (August 3, 2006).
2. Jennifer Dunning, *Alvin Ailey: A Life in Dance* (New York: Da Capo Press, 1998), p. 275.
3. E. Jean Carroll, "Justify Your Love," *Elle Magazine*, February 2001, <http://www.ejeanlive.com/madonna.htm> (August 7, 2006).
4. Christopher Anderson, "Madonna Rising: The Wild and Funky Early Years in New York," *New York Magazine*, October 14, 1991.
5. "Self-guided Walking Tour Around East Campus," n.d., <http://www.owdna.org/tour.htm> (September 28, 2005).

Chapter 8. **Gambler**

1. Barbara Victor, *Goddess: Inside Madonna* (New York: Harper Collins, Inc, 2001), p. 179.
2. Masha Leon, *Forward*, April 15, 1994, vol. LXXXXVII, iss. 30,971, p.2.
3. Andrew Morton, *Madonna* (New York: St. Martin's Press, 2001), p. 65.
4. Ibid., p. 66.
5. Victor.

Chapter 9. **Born to Be Alive**

1. "Artist Biographies: Patrick Hernandez," *Disco Museum website*, n.d., <http://www.discomuseum.com/PatrickHernandez.html> (September 28, 2005).
2. "Gloria Gaynor website," n.d., <http://www.gloria-gaynor.com/> (September 28, 2005).
3. "Artist Biographies: Patrick Hernandez," *Disco Museum website*.
4. Ibid.

Chapter 10. Madonna in the Sky

1. Andrew Morton, *Madonna* (St. Martin's Press: New York, 2001), p. 80.
2. Ibid., p. 81.
3. Christopher Anderson, "Madonna Rising: The Wild and Funky Early Years in New York," *New York Magazine*, October 14, 1991.
4. Neil Strauss, "How Madonna Got Her Groove Back," *Rolling Stone Magazine*, December 1, 2005.

Chapter 11. Right on Track

1. Bob Grossweiner and Jane Cohen, "Industry Profile: Camille Barbone," *CelebrityAcess* © *2001–2006 Gen-Den Corporation*, <http://www.celebrityaccess.com/news/profile.html?id=280> (July 19, 2006).
2. Andrew Morton, *Madonna* (St. Martin's Press: New York, 2001), p. 92.
3. Christopher Connelly, "Madonna Goes All the Way," *Rolling Stone Magazine*, November 22, 1984.
4. Bob Grossweiner and Jane Cohen, "Industry Profile: Camille Barbone."
5. "Gonna make a move that knocks you over/Watch this turn one's gonna put you away," *Breakfast Club Lyrics: Right on Track*, <http://www.lyricsondemand.com/b/breakfastclublyrics/rightontracklyrics.html> (September 28, 2005).

Chapter 12. Everybody, Everybody

1. Jeanette Walls, "Madonna Pushes Friends to the Borderline," *MSNBC*, May 10, 2004, <http://msnbc.msn.com/id/4926130/> (July 29, 2006).
2. Frank Owen, *Clubland: The Fabulous Rise and Murderous Fall of Club Culture* (New York, St. Martin's Press, 2003).
3. "Madonna: She's One Lucky Star!," *Teen Magazine*, 1984.

4. Simon Frith, "The Sound of Erotica: Pain, Power, and Pop," in Lisa Frank and Paul Smith, *Madonnarama: Essays on Sex and Popular Culture* (Pennsylvania: Cleis Press, 1993).

5. "Madonna and Child, The New Baby, The New Life," *Vanity Fair*, March 1998, <http://www.fortunecity. com/tinpan/underworld/437/vf.htm> (September 28, 2005).

6. Andrew Morton, *Madonna* (St. Martin's Press: New York, 2001), p. 104.

7. Owen.

8. "Mark Kamins: Legendary USA Disc Jockey," *DJ Portal*, September 20, 2003, <http://djsportal.com/en/ pioneer/index.php?id=mark> (September 28, 2005).

Chapter 13. Starlight, Star Bright

1. Keith Haring, "Conversations with Fred Brathwaite, Fred Schneider, Jellybean Benitez and Junior Vasquez," *The Keith Haring Foundation*, n.d., <http://www.haring. com/cgi-bin/essays.cgi?essay_id=07> (September 28, 2005).

Chapter 14. Keep on Pushin' Me

1. "Madonna: Five professional collaborations that carried on in the bedroom...," *Top of the Pops 2—Top 5*, n.d., <http://www.bbc.co.uk/totp2/features/top5/ madonna.shtml> (August 4, 2006).

2. Pamela Robertson, "Guilty Pleasures," *Guilty Pleasures: Feminist Camp from Mae West to Madonna* (Duke University Press, 1996), p. 123.

3. "MTV News; Madonna Raw—The Early Years," n.d., <http://www.fortunecity.com/tinpan/underworld/ 437/raw.htm> (September 28, 2005).

4. Ibid.

5. Christopher Connelly, "Madonna Goes All the Way," *Rolling Stone Magazine*, November 22, 1984.

Chapter 15. Burning Up

1. "MTV News; Madonna Raw—The Early Years," n.d., <http://www.fortunecity.com/tinpan/underworld/437/raw.htm> (September 28, 2005).
2. Andrew Morton, *Madonna* (St. Martin's Press: New York, 2001), p. 126.
3. Becky Johnston, "Confession of a Catholic School Girl," *Interview Magazine*, 1989.
4. Ibid.
5. "MTV News; Madonna Raw—The Early Years."
6. Roger Ebert, *Desperately Seeking Susan Review*, March 29, 1985, <http://rogerebert.suntimes.com/apps/pbcs.dll/article?AID=/19850329/REVIEWS/503290301/1023> (September 28, 2005).

Chapter 16. Why's It So Hard

1. Pamela Robertson, *Guilty Pleasures: Feminist Camp from Mae West to Madonna*, (Durham, N.C.: Duke University Press), 1996, p. 127.
2. "MTV News; Madonna Raw—The Early Years" <http://www.fortunecity.com/tinpan/underworld/437/raw.htm>
3. Andrew Morton, *Madonna*, (St. Martin's Press: New York, 2001), p. 126
4. "Sean Penn—Madonna Would Have Ruined My life," *Britain Now Magazine*, April 21, 2005, <http://www.femalefirst.co.uk/celebrity/36042004.htm> (September 28, 2005).
5. Michael Goldberg, "Performance Review: Madonna Seduces Seattle," *Rolling Stone Magazine*, May 23, 1985.
6. Becky Johnston, "Confession of a Catholic School Girl," *Interview Magazine*, 1989.
7. Madonna, *Live: The Virgin Tour*, 1985 Boy Toy, Inc.

Chapter 17. Poison Penns

1. Richard T. Kelly, *Sean Penn: His Life and Times* (New York: Canongate U.S., 2004), p. 217.

2. Ibid., p. 158.

3. "Madonna's Road to Matrimony Wasn't Studded With Success," *Sky News-London*, January 24, 2001, <http://www.foxnews.com/story/0,2933,606,00.html> (September 28, 2005).

4. Andrew Morton, *Madonna* (New York: St. Martin's Press, 2001), p. 138.

5. Kelly, p. 161.

6. Bill Zehme, "Madonna," *Rolling Stone Magazine*, March 23, 1989.

7. "Sean Penn—Madonna Would Have Ruined My life," *Britain Now Magazine*, April 21, 2005, <http://www.femalefirst.co.uk/celebrity/36042004.htm> (September 25, 2005).

8. Stephen Holden, "Madonna Goes Heavy on Heart," *New York Times*, June 29, 1986.

9. Greg Kot, "Without the videos, her albums just aren't the same," *Chicago Tribune*, May 13, 1990.

10. Robert Hilburn, "Madonna Is Nobody's Toy," *Los Angeles Times*, July 6, 1986.

11. Michael Gilmore, "The Madonna Mystique," *Rolling Stone Magazine*, September 10, 1987.

12. Ibid.

13. Morton, p. 143.

Chapter 18. I Can Feel Your Power

1. "Music, Myth and Controversy," *Songtalk Magazine*, 1989, <http://www.madonnavillage.com/library/interviews/songtalk1989.html> (September 28, 2005).

2. J.D. Considine, "Madonna's True Confessions," *Rolling Stone Magazine*, April 6, 1989.

3. "Music, Myth and Controversy," *Songtalk Magazine*.

4. Bill Zehme, "Madonna," *Rolling Stone Magazine*, March 23, 1989.

5. C.W. Arrington, "Madonna is in Bloom: Circe at Loom," *TIME*, Vol. 137, Issue 20, May 20, 1991.

6. "Music, Myth and Controversy," *Songtalk Magazine*.

7. "Madonna and Child: The New Baby, the New Life," *Vanity Fair*, March 1998, <http://www.fortunecity.com/tinpan/underworld/437/vf.htm#> (September 28, 2005).

8. Fraser Boa, *The Way of Myth: Talking With Joseph Campbell* (Boston, Mass.: Shambhala Publications, 1994).

9. Becky Johnston, "Confessions of a Catholic School Girl," *Interview Magazine*, 1989.

10. Carla Freccero, "Our Lady of MTV: Madonna's 'Like a Prayer,'" *boundary 2*, Duke University Press, Summer 1992.

11. Elizabeth Tippens, "Mastering Madonna," *Rolling Stone Magazine*, September 17, 1992.

12. Camille Paglia, "Venus of the Radio Waves," *Sex, Art and American Culture* (New York: Vintage Books, 1992), p. 11.

Chapter 19. Live Out Your Fantasies Here With Me

1. AbsoluteMadonna.com, "Blond Ambition Tour 1990," <http://www.absolutemadonna.com/tours/ba.shtml> (August 4, 2006).

2. Don Shewey, "Madonna: The Saint, the Slut, the Sensation," *The Advocate*, 1991, <http://www.donshewey.com/music_articles/madonna1.htm> (July 19, 2006).

3. Alek Keshishian, *Truth or Dare*, Boy Toy Productions/Miramax Films, 1991.

4. Don Shewey, "Madonna: The Saint, the Slut, the Sensation."

5. "Vanilla Ice," n.d., <http://en.wikipedia.org/wiki/Vanilla_Ice> (January 7, 2006).

6. Bell Hooks, "Madonna: Plantation Mistress or Soul Sister?" in *Black Looks: Race and Representation* (London: Turnaround, 1992).

7. Douglas Crimp and Michael Warner, "No sex in *Sex*" in Lisa Frank and Paul Smith, *Madonnarama: Essays on Sex and Popular Culture* (San Francisco: Cleis Press, 1993), p. 95.
8. Ibid.
9. Ibid.

Chapter 20. **A League of Her Own**

1. Douglas Crimp and Michael Warner, "No sex in *Sex*" in Lisa Frank and Paul Smith, *Madonnarama: Essays on Sex and Popular Culture* (San Francisco: Cleis Press, 1993), p. 100.
2. Don Romesburg, "Madonna Dares," *The Advocate*, May 11, 1999.
3. Peter Wilkinson, "Madonna's Favorite Filmmaker Is One Smart Alek," *Rolling Stone Magazine*, May 16, 1991.
4. Ibid.
5. "In Bed With Madonna/*Truth or Dare* film review," *New Internationalist*, August 1991, <http://www.newint.org/issue222/reviews.htm> (January 6, 2006).
6. Don Shewey, "Madonna: The Saint, the Slut, the Sensation," *The Advocate*, 1991, <http://www.donshewey.com/music_articles/madonna1.htm> (July 19, 2006).
7. Crimp and Warner, "No sex in *Sex*."
8. Wilkinson.
9. "Dita Parlo," n.d., <http://en.wikipedia.org/wiki/Dita_Parlo> (September 28, 2005).
10. Madonna, *Sex* (New York: Warner Books, 1992).
11. Carol A. Queen, "Talking About *Sex*" in Lisa Frank and Paul Smith, *Madonnarama: Essays on Sex and Popular Culture* (San Francisco: Cleis Press, 1993), p. 143.

Chapter 21. **You Must Love Me**

1. Mim Udovitch, "Madonna," *US Magazine*, January 1997.
2. Ibid.

3. Janet Maslin, "Dangerous Game," *New York Times*, 1993, <http://movies2.nytimes.com/gst/movies/movie.html?v_id=123054> (January 6, 2006).

4. Carol A. Queen, "Talking About *Sex*" in Lisa Frank and Paul Smith, *Madonnarama: Essays on Sex and Popular Culture* (San Francisco: Cleis Press, 1993), p. 145.

5. Ibid.

6. Angie Hung, "High Flying Adored: Madonnatribe Meets Tim Rice," 2005, <http://www.madonnatribe.com/idol/timrice.htm> (September 28, 2005).

7. Udovitch.

8. Ibid.

9. Ibid.

Chapter 22. Open Your Heart to Me

1. Andrew Morton, *Madonna* (New York: St. Martin's Press, 2001), p. 213.

2. Larry King, "Madonna Reviews Life," *Larry King Live*, <http://www.cnn.com/SHOWBIZ/Music/9901/19/madonna.lkl/> (July 19, 2006).

3. Danny Eccleston, "Confessions of the World's Most Famous Woman," *Q Magazine*, 1998, <http://www.madonnavillage.com/library/interviews/q1998.html> (August 4, 2006).

4. Ingrid Sischy, "Madonna and Child: The New Baby, the New Life," *Vanity Fair*, 1998, <http://www.fortunecity.com/tinpan/underworld/437/vf.htm> (September 28, 2005).

5. Barry Walter, "Madonna Just Made Her Most Daring Album in Years," *Spin Magazine*, 1998, <http://www.madonna-online.ch/m-online/interviews/interview-sites/98-04_spin-interview.htm> (September 28, 2005).

6. Don Shewey, "The Saint, the Slut," *The Advocate*, 1991, <http://www.donshewey.com/music_articles/madonna1.htm> (August 4, 2006).

7. Miranda Sawyer, "It's My Love You But F*** You Record," *The Face*, 2000, <http://www.madonnavillage. com/library/interviews/theface2000.html> (August 7, 2006).

8. Ibid.

9. Morton, p. 231.

10. Dubbed "Holy Spice," she is the first female minister in the United Kingdom in charge of a cathedral. Jill Smolowe, Pete Norman, Joanne Fowler, Caris Davis, et al., "Kilt by Association," *People Weekly*, Jan 8, 2001, Vol.55, Issue. 1; p. 44.

11. Barbara Victor, *Goddess: Inside Madonna* (New York: Harper Collins, 2001), p. 375.

12. Jill Smolowe, Pete Norman, Joanne Fowler, Caris Davis, et al., "Kilt by Association."

13. Ibid.

Chapter 23. **Time Goes So Slowly**

1. Barry Walter, "Madonna Just Made Her Most Daring Album in Years," *Spin Magazine*, <http://www.madonna-online.ch/m-online/interviews/interview-sites/98-04_spin-interview.htm> (July 19, 2006).

2. Alex Needham, "Madonna: London Earl's Court," *NME*, 2001, <http://www.madonna-online.ch/m-online/tours/01_dwt/reviews/dwt-reviews.htm> (July 19, 2006).

3. "Crazy Jamie: MadonnaTribe meets Jamie King," *MaddonaTribe*, 2005, <http://www.madonnatribe.com/idol/jamie_one.htm> (July 19, 2006).

4. "Crazy Jamie: MadonnaTribe meets Jamie King," *MaddonaTribe*.

5. Corey Moss, "Madonna Twirls Rifle, Lifts Up Her Kilt at Opener," *MTV News Archive*, May 25, 2004, <http://www.mtv.com/news/articles/1487434/20040525/nullmadonna.html> (January 6, 2006).

6. "A Madonna Discography, 2001–2006," n.d., <http://www.matthewhunt.com/madonna/tours.html> (July 29, 2006).

7. John Wiederhorn, "Madonna Yanks Controversial American Life Video," *MTV.com*, March 31, 2003, <http://www.mtv.com/news/articles/1470876/20030331/madonna.jhtml?headlines=true> (July 19, 2006).

8. Russ Kick, "Images from 'American Life,' the Video Madonna Won't Release," *The Memory Hole*, April 4, 2003, <http://www.thememoryhole.org/arts/american-life.htm> (September 28, 2005).

9. Harry Smith, "Madonna: Being Onstage a Battle," *The Early Show*, Dec. 21, 2004, <http://www.cbsnews.com/stories/2004/12/21/earlyshow/leisure/celebspot/main662223.shtml> (September 28, 2005).

10. "Material Girl Goes from Madonna to Esther: Singer Adopts Hebrew Name as a Way to Show Interest in Kabbalah," June 18, 2004, <http://www.msnbc.msn.com/id/5234922/> (January 6, 2006).

11. Harry Smith, "Madonna: Diva, Author, Housewife," *The Early Show*, n.d., <http://www.cbsnews.com/stories/2004/12/20/earlyshow/leisure/celebspot/main661931.shtml> (September 28, 2005).

12. Karen Springen, "Writing Dynamo: Children's Author Jane Yolen has published nearly 300 books, but she's got plenty more stories to tell," August 12, 2005, <http://www.msnbc.msn.com/id/8917828/site/newsweek/> (January 6, 2006).

13. Barry Walter, "Madonna Just Made Her Most Daring Album in Years."

14. Terri Gross, "Madonna: Pop Icon, Children's Writer," *Fresh Air from WHYY*, November 23, <http://www.npr.org/templates/story/story.php?storyId=4183844&sourceCode=RSS> (January 6, 2006).

15. "Entertainment Briefs," n.d., <http://cbs2chicago.com/entertainmentbriefs/ARCHIVE/20051020/resources_entertainment_html> (January 6, 2006).

16. Absolute Madonna website, n.d., <http://www.absolutemadonna.com/tours/confessions.shtml> (January 6, 2006).

17. Rachel Sanderson, "Rome Church condemns Madonna's crucifixion stunt," *Yahoo! News*, August 3, 2006, <http://news.yahoo.com/s/nm/20060803/people_nm/madonna_crucifixion_dc;_ylt=AjA6Oq7gWeWCrJd6CuYj EgdxFb8C;_ylu=X3oD...> (August 31, 2006).

18. Stephen M. Silverman, "German Prosecutors Eye Madonna Concert," *People.com*, August 16, 2006, <http://people.aol.com/people/article/0,26334,1227338,00.html> (August 31, 2006).

19. Reuters, "Madonna's Rome Concert Outrages Vatican," *People.com*, August 7, 2006, <http://people.aol/com/people/article/0,26334,1223466,00.html> (August 31, 2006).

20. "Madonna to Help Orphaned Children in Africa," *People.com*, August 3, 2006, <http://people.aol.com/people/article/0,26334,1222452,00.html> (August 31, 2006).

21. Ibid.

22. Ibid.

23. Ibid.

24. Merle Ginsberg, "Madonna: The Saga Continues," n.d., <http://www.style.com/w/feat_story/031203/full_page.html> (January 6, 2006).

Further Reading

Books

Feinstein, Stephen. *The 1980s From Ronald Reagan to MTV, Revised Edition*. Berkeley Heights, N.J.: Enslow Publishers, Inc., 2006.

Koopmans, Andy. *Madonna*. San Diego, Calif.: Lucent Books, 2003.

Orgill, Roxane. *Shout, Sister, Shout!: Ten Girl Singers Who Shaped a Century*. New York: Margaret K. McElderry Books, 2001.

Wheeler, Jill C. *Madonna*. Edina, Minn.: ABDO & Daughters, 2003.

Madonna's Books For Children

Madonna. *The English Roses*. New York: Callaway Editions, 2003.

Madonna. *Mr. Peabody's Apples*. New York: Callaway Editions, 2003.

Madonna. *Yakov and the Seven Thieves*. New York: Callaway Editions, 2004.

Madonna. *The Adventures of Abdi*. New York: Callaway Editions, 2004.

Madonna. *Lotsa de Casha*. New York: Callaway Editions, 2005.

Internet Addresses

Madonna

<http://www.madonna.com>

Visit the official Madonna Web site.

Madonna

<http://www.madonnalicious.com>

This fan site about Madonna has some of the latest information about the star.

Index

A

Aguilera, Christina, 11, **12**, 14
AIDS awareness, 80, 105–106
A League of Their Own, 113
Alter, Adam, 60–61
Alvin Ailey American Dance Theatre, 44–45
American Dance Festival, 46, 47
American Life (album), 13, 22, 26
"American Life" (song), 129, 130
Arquette, Rosanna, 76–77, 87

B

Barbone, Camille, 60–62
Bedtime Stories, 113
Bell, Erica, 65, 71, 87
Benitez, John "Jellybean," 68–71, 80
Berg, Michael, 136
"Blond Ambition," 25, 100–103, 107, 134
Borderline, 71–72
Bowie, David, 9, 74
Bray, Stephen, 44, 59, 61–63, 74–75
Breakfast Club, 57–58, 62
Burke, Gary, 58–59, 61–62
"Burning Up," 63, 68, 71

C

Catholicism, 18, 22, 30, 32, 49, 94–95, 96–98, 102, 121–122, 124, 134–135
children's books, 131–**133**

Ciccone, Anthony (brother), 23, 34
Ciccone, Christopher (brother), 23, 25, 29, 42, 71, 100, 105, **108**, 109, 114
Ciccone, Jennifer (half sister), 29
Ciccone Leon, Lourdes "Lola" Maria (daughter), 11, 13, 25, 82, 117–119, 121, 123, 124, 131
Ciccone, Madonna Louise. *See* Madonna
Ciccone, Mario (half brother), 29
Ciccone, Martin (brother), 23
Ciccone, Melanie (sister), 23, 24–25
Ciccone, Paula (sister), 23, 87
Ciccone, Silvio (father), 22–24, 27–28, 30, **31**–34, 38, 44, 93, 132
Confessions on a Dance Floor, 59, 126, 134

D

Dangerous Game, 113
DeMann, Freddy, 69–71, 76–77
Desperately Seeking Susan, 76–77
Dick Tracy, 78, 102–103
disco, 41, 51–55, 61, 64, 68, 71, 91, 103, 126, 134
Dress You Up, 83–84
"Drowned World," 127–129
Duke University, 38, 46–49

E

"Easy Ride," 22
Emmy, 59–61
Erotica (album), 38, 113
"Erotica" (song), 105, 111
"Everybody," 63, 65–68, 71
Evita, 19, 78, 103, 114–116

F

Flynn, Christopher, 37–38,
  40–44, 46, 56, 105
Fortin, Dale (uncle), 23
Fortin, Elsie (grandmother),
  24, 30
Fortin Ciccone, Madonna
  (mother), 22–26, 93

G

Gilroy, Dan, 56–59, 62
Gilroy, Ed, 56–59
"Girlie Show," 114
Golden Globe Awards, 116,
Gotham Sound Studios,
  60–62, 64
Graham, Martha, 16, 45,
  47–48
Grammy Awards, 8, **120**, 121
Gustafson, Joan (stepmother),
  28, 31

H

"Has to Be," 122
Hernandez, Patrick, 51–56
homosexuality, 9, 14, 18,
  40–42, 44, 103–107, 109,
  129

I

I'm Breathless, 103
"In This Life," 38

J

Jackson, Michael, 8, 9, 40,
  69, 91
"Justify My Love," 105

K

Kabbalah, 121, 130, 131,
  136
Kamins, DJ Mark, 66–67
Keshishian, Alex, **108**, 109

L

Lambert, Mary, 71, 82, 96
Lang, Pearl, 45–51, 53
Leon, Carlos, 117–119, 126
Let Me Tell You a Secret,
  133–134
Like a Prayer, 27, 75, 92, 93,
  96–99
"Like a Virgin," 9, 11, 74,
  102
Live–Aid, 80, **81**, 106
"Lucky Star," 68, 71

M

Madonna, **10**, **12**, **35**, **39**,
  80, **84**, **90**, **92**, **108**, **120**,
  125, **133**
  ballet, 37–44, 48
  childhood and family life,
    22–34
  controversy, 12, 13, 15, 19,
    32, 112, 130, 135
  early career, 51–66
  education, 43–44, 46
  feminism, 18–19, 23, 91,
    104
  high school, 34, **35**, 36–37,
    39, 43–44
  marriages, 86–89, 93,
    122–126
  motherhood, 117–119, 124,
    131
  reinvention, 16–17,
    130–131
  religion. *See* Catholicism;
    Kabbalah

sexuality, 14, 18, 30, 42, 72, 95, 101, 102, 105, 134
style, 65–66, 83, 85, 101
Madonna and the Sky, 58
"Material Girl" (song), 78
Material Girl (video), 82
Maverick Entertainment, 110, 112–113
Maverick Records, 113
Mazar, Debi, 63, 65, 87, 103, 126
"Mer Girl," 25–26
Millionaires. *See* Emmy
Monahan, Mike, 58
Monroe, Marilyn, 79
"Mother and Father," 26
MTV, 8, 10, 11, 12, 15, 72, 74, 76, 80, 101, 130
Music, 121, 123, 128
music videos, 70–73

O
Orbit, William, 119, 121

P
Paglia, Camille, 15, 98
Papa Don't Preach, 27, 29, 31, 82, 91
paparazzi, 83, 86–88
Parker, Alan, 115–116
Penn, Sean, 82–83, **84**, 86–89, 92
"Promise to Try," 27
"protean style," 16–17

R
Raising Malawi project, 136
Ray of Light, 25, 119, **120**, 122, 127
"Re–Invention" tour, 128–130, 133
Rice, Time, 115–116
Ritchie, Guy (husband), 86, 122–**125**, 126
Ritchie, Rocco (son), 124, **125**, 131
"Rock N Roll Circus," 128
Rodgers, Nile, 74
Rolling Stone magazine, 19, 61, 72, 83

S
Sex, 19, 110–114
Shadows and Fog, 113
Sire Records, 66–69, 71
Spears, Britney, 11, **12**, 13, 14, 19–20

T
True Blue, 82, 89
Truth or Dare, 25, 78, 107, **108**–110, 133

V
Video Music Awards (VMA), 8–9, **10**, 11–13, 15
Virgin Tour, 32, 80, 85
"Vogue," 103

W
"What it Feels Like for a Girl," 18–19
Who's That Girl, 82, **90**–92